Change to Shame

Change to Shame

Valarie Kent Fringero

Library of Congress Control Number: 2010917884
ISBN: Softcover   978-1-4568-0989-8
               Ebook   978-1-4568-0990-4

To order additional copies of this book, contact:
Xlibris Corporation
1-888-795-4274
www.Xlibris.com
Orders@Xlibris.com
89056

This book is dedicated to my parents with love

Ruthie Kent
Willie Kent

I love you too much!

Well, khow is your family?

Do you come for a large family?

In my story it does not matter the size of the family. The love and how much you value one another the moral fiber of family the weight of the truth is what matter. The real love you share for each other which no outsider can ever come between.

I'm sure at one time or another everyone has lost someone prominent in their life. That could be a Mother, Father, sister, brother, uncle, aunt, close friend anyone that holds that place in your heart.

For me I cherish my family. I love everyone I have come to know. I respect people it don't matter what hand life has dealt you or the color of your skin. Everyone has feeling some people show them and some hide them. Me it don't matter I try to keep it real what you see is what you get.

In my life I have lost so many and only God knows the reason why. See most people get things mixed up the way a person die is not the reason they died. I believe that god has a direct plan for everyone life, death, rich, poor, health, sickness its' all in the plan.

Although we are never ready for death even if we know that it's coming we're never ready. What can you do its life and weather we want it or not we all have to go that same route some day. I do believe where we go does depend on how we live our life how we treat people in our everyday life.

See I come from a family of 10 and I fit in the middle. I guess you can call that a large family. I was born on the west side of Chicago my parents were Willie & Ruthie Kent I have always been engorged with love from family and friends. Although life in a big family hasn't always been all good we have fight arguments lie on one another you know the works growing up in a real dysfunctional family and that's what my family is loving but dysfunctional. Especially without my parents. When I think back one of the things I remember is growing up on the west side of Chicago. All the people in my neighborhood The Moody's, The Skies, the Johnsons' the families on the block were wonderful they were like family everybody looked out for each other and all the kids too. If you did something wrong the neighbor would beat your butt and take you home then your ma-ma would get you and when your father came home there goes another so you dare not do any thing bad. It's like the old saying it takes a neighbor to raise a child . . . if children were raised like that today we might not have so many teen deaths.

I have 3 sisters Stacy the oldest of the family Sue who is known as the crazy girl Diane the baby girl that shows that she is the baby all the time you know my way or no way. Next there are my brothers Tommy who is next to the oldest David the loner all he wants' to do is fix things but the truth is he brakes more than he fix then there's Will spoil cheater liar that boy can't tell the truth to save his life. Lil Man he is so cute and he's' just good all he does is follow ma-ma and sit on the floor by her and rub her legs. I think he likes the fill of her stockings and the other two don't do nothing I guess that's because their still babies.

My family originates from Mississippi my mother and father migrated to the west side of Chicago in the 1950's in search of a new beginning. Something different from the old south in which they we're made to live in segregation, racial injustice, picking cotton, inadequate housing amongst many other black and white issues in the time. Daddy was 16 years old when he first came to Chicago in 1952

Once here Daddy found a job with jitney cab co. Later he began to work for Ogden metal Co. as a truck driver but Daddy had a guitar and he had it in his head that he would become famous like some of the people he grew up listening to on the King Biscuit Time radio show that aired out of Helena Arkansas in the south back then you didn't have nothing but radio and that's if you were lucky. Daddy would sneak to the juke joint at night when grand ma was asleep and peer in thru the window to hear those men play and make that blues music the music that would stir his soul for the rest of his life. While in Chicago he would go to every club he could he was too young to be in the club but that didn't stop him. So every night after work he would go to juke joints with his guitar and hope some one would let him play.

Daddy would go to those clubs no matter how tired he was daddy was determined to make it.

Finally one night he was at this joint named Sylvio's.

He started playing by sitting in with a friend's band.

Daddy played lead guitar and switching to bass . . . see he was kind of tricked into it when the bassist would show up drunk too drunk to play and daddy found his self quickly in demand on the bass that's how daddy started playing the bass full time eventually backing up Chicago blues greats like Little Walter, Muddy Waters, Howlin Wolf and more. Daddy's guitar playing took a detour for the better.

Ma-Ma would tell daddy he was doing too much but it's what daddy wanted to do and he wasn't going to stop until he got what he wanted.

Daddy fell in love with the bass he still loved a good lead guitar don't get me wrong but daddy had a unique sound on the bass he just got better and better as his sound matured his voice was transcending people began to talk of him more and more he began to get more gigs it wasn't a lot of bass players in that time but he was the best. See everybody wanted to play the lead guitar to be the man. Daddy wanted it to at one time but he got more work and recognitions playing the bass and that worked out good daddy was a country man not a dumb man.

Daddy played all over the Chicago up & down Madison you name it he played it.

This went on for about 10 or 12 years daddy went on his first real tour outside the states in 1970s the band he played with was opening act for B.B. King on a regular basis. Things really picked up for daddy he did a lot of opening for famous people he was working every night.

Later daddy had a falling out with the band leader while overseas that was it when Daddy got back home he quit this band and that's when Daddy formed his own band.

It came pretty easy for daddy to form his own band because he was known on the blues scene as the best bass player and everyone knew he was a good and fair man he would pay the guys that worked in his band very well even if he even if it cost him to be short on his money he should have cleared.

While getting the band together and taking dates for gigs daddy had to hurry up and come up with a name for his band one day we were in the kitchen eating breakfast daddy ma-ma and myself daddy looked at ma-ma and ask Ruth what do you think would be a good name for my band? He was sitting at the table. I looked at daddy and said ooh I know what about the jam band! I was all excited. Daddy looked at me and said we can't use that baby that isn't good with a smile on his face. Then ma-ma said I got a name for you Willie what about Sugar Bear this is a name she use to tease daddy with all the time around the house then daddy said ok, now what about the guys what will I call them? The Beehives then daddy ok that sound catchy I think its sounds good, well I will go with that for now I will tell the guys tonight. But you should think about using your own name ma-ma said. daddy went along Sugar bear & the Beehives for a while later we (the kids) came up with Willie Kent & the Gent's and daddy loved it he said it had a certain ring to it so it's been that every since.

Ma-Ma made a good point to daddy by using his name everyone would know who he was. Now as things progress it came to be that

The world knew my daddy he did get what he wanted with one exception but he did get 10 W.C. Handy blues Award's, Lifetime achievement award, Album of the year award among other's he had signed with several records companies. look at it this is a remarkable achievement for a cotton picker from down in the Delta but Daddy wanted a Grammy for one piece of his work and believe me its' worth it ! Daddy didn't get a Grammy but his achievements will never be matched. One other thing he wanted and that was that people would always remember him. Today people still talk about daddy in good reference to him as a good man, friend. I know he got his Grammy and rememberance, reward's in heaven

I am so very proud of him and to say Willie Kent is my father.

My mother was from Jackson Miss. Her mother died after ma-ma was born she died from child birth ma-ma aunt raised her when ma-ma was about 15 years old they moved to Chicago ma-ma went to school on the west side she would walk to school everyday and that is how she met Daddy.

Daddy was a cab driver for a short while when he first came to Chicago so he drove all over the city he would see ma-ma going to school everyday when he saw her for the first time he was hooked and he took the same route everyday at the same time so he could see her. He finally got up the nerve to approach her and wouldn't stop until he got her to go out on a date with him. This is the beginning of the Kent family our story. They dated for a little while then they married and in a period of exactly nine months after they meet they had their first child it was a girl my big sister 11 months later another my big brother then another and the babies just kept on coming until there was 10 children.

Now at this time ma-ma and daddy had to work hard what ever job they could get to support all of us now with daddy working two jobs ma-ma had to find some work she did a lot of odd jobs' just to make end's meet ma-ma always like doing hair she had heard from her girlfriend that she could get a job at this funeral home over on Jackson Blvd. named Biggs &Biggs so ma-ma went over there and she got the job styling the hair of the dead. But that didn't last long because daddy didn't like her working there around dead when ma-ma would come home from work daddy would stand far away from her while talking with her and teasing her about working at this place with dead folks as he would put it but all the time he didn't like it one bit. He would complain to her every day about doing that kind of work one day they had an argument because daddy told ma-ma to quit. if I quit what will you have me do I have to work somewhere so I can take care of the kids ma-ma said I don't care where you work, but not there, I don't want you doing that I know you can find another job somewhere daddy said. Well just stay home and take care of the kids and the house until you find something I just don't want you doing that I didn't say I don't want you to work I really don't want you working there o-k Ruth daddy said. That was that so now daddy starting teaching ma-ma how to drive so she could go to find a better job and be able to take us to our clinic appointment with out him missing work so once he was sure that ma-ma could drive well he came home one day and surprised her with a car daddy bought ma-ma a little blue car. Why did he do that?

Ma-ma was a road runner she would not stay out of that car once she learned how to drive she would load us up in that car and we would go everywhere. We were never at home until it was time for her to get dinner ready. Then she found a job at some company and she liked it. Ma-ma would come home from work and cook dinner Ma-ma was one of the best cook in the world and I'm not just saying that because she was my mother she could cook anything and it would be the ultimate in dinning. Ma-ma would cook and put people to shame with her cooking I had a girlfriend that got smack in the mouth by her mother for saying that she didn't want to eat her mothers sweet potatoes because they didn't taste good like my ma-ma's and that is the god's honest truth !!

Ma-ma was a good mother she would make sure the family would eat on time we got to school everyday and the laundry was done, the house was clean then on top of that she would go to work she was incredible, we never missed a Sunday school lesson ma-ma was a Sunday school teacher. One day ma-ma came home early from work she was sitting in the living room with one of her friends Marie I was in the kitchen looking in the refrigerator and I heard her tell her friend that her job had closed they were no longer in business and now she didn't know what to do. I don't know how we were going to make it now I have to let Willie know when he get home I don't know how he is going to take this things were just beginning to look up well you know do better. Well I got to tell him any way. Ma-ma's strong will came through again. She didn't stop until she found work. She starting working at this place called sweetheart cup co. I think she made lot's more money because every Saturday when ma-ma wasn't working she would gather us all up and away we would go in that little car to the suburbs shopping and eating at all the restaurant and donut shops it was wonderful times we looked forward to Saturday with her. ma-ma would make sure we as kids would see more than the neighborhood in which we lived and knew more than our race of people as we grew we had a number of different nationality of friends that would come over our house and sleep over (only so they could eat) no I'm just kidding they were good friends but they did like to eat ma-ma cooking hell who didn't?

Then one day out of the blue Daddy & Ma-ma called us all in the living room our living room was big and covered in gold and black velvet wall paper right off the living room was ma-ma and daddy's bedroom as you walk back there was the front door then you were in the kitchen to the right was the back door on the left was two bedroom my sisters and I shared the one room and my brothers the other we all had bunk beds down from the rooms was the bathroom and the washer and dryer was in the hall the house wasn't that big but it was full with love. Ma-ma and daddy wanted to talk to us they ask how would like to have your own bedroom? We're all looking at each other with a puzzled look on our faces.

Then ma-ma (while pointing at my big sister) what about you? Your own back yard? (At this time my big sister was pregnant) Then Ma-ma said let's tell them Willie

Ma-ma said we're moving your daddy and I bought a house!! What a house! Stacy shouted.

We were all excited and there were so many questions where is it? What color is it? Is it big? The questions were flying all over the place but once it set in it got kind of quiet because that meant we would be leaving all of our friends.

But it got better we still had each other and we were really close as a family. And we could always make new friends that's one of the things ma-ma instill in us ma-ma gave us good direction the right morals ma-ma was a good person and her heart was filled with love and she was good unless you made her not so good.

Ma-ma was not afraid to show you the other side of her hand if you know what I mean.

To know her is to love her ask anyone that knew Ma-ma they'll tell you the same she was a lovely person inside and out beautiful skin, color, hair, personality ma-ma looked like a Indian and everyone she met was a friend she didn't meet no strangers. ma-ma would help everyone she could that's the kind of love she was filled with unconditional but if she thought you could do better she would tell you to get some order about yourself that's because she knew you could do better.

Ma-ma believes that there was no such thing as people that fail but the failer in a person for lack of trying.

When we mover to our new house on the south side of Chicago it is a big beautiful brick house and it has lots of room a front porch with a yard a big back yard where we can play three bathrooms one on every floor a den, living room, dinning room, basement it's a dream house I felt like we were rich we've never lived in something like this before! Things got better and better ma-ma had a good job the music business had picked up for daddy tremendously the neighborhood was great although we were the only black family living in the area the schools were good it was good and my family only got closer. We played together went to school together we did everything together we were tighter than ever the family stayed that way and the holidays were unbelievable the house would be filled with friends and family not to mention all of us kids and Christmas was like story book our lives had taking such a divine turn to it no one would believe we were children of cotton pickers.

Ma-ma bought this big wicker chair and it would sit in the dinning room along the wall by the flowers that were in a wicker vase and every day we would take pictures one of us all of us it didn't matter we just took pictures. Daddy always kept us a pet mainly dogs we had a beautiful dog his name was fluffy he was golden brown in color and his hair was thick and wavy he was a very smart dog fluffy wouldn't let any one do any harm to us. One day we let Fluffy out like we always did he would go and take a leak and come right back to the house this day Fluffy didn't come back so we went out to look for him. down by the corner store there were a lot of people gathered when we got there if was fluffy just lying there we started crying hard the family was so hurt when daddy came home he went to find out what happen he came in the house and talked to us and said that fluffy had been poison and that he would get us another dog and not to cry but we couldn't help it he was like a part of the family.

My daddy kept his word like he always done if daddy said he was going to do something you could bet your life he was going to do it that's the kind of man my daddy was. The next dog daddy got us was a German Sheppard we named him Smooth and over time he got big he was black with tan on his paws and a little tan on his chest and his coat would just shine Daddy said we had to feed him eggs to keep his coat shiny Smooth was a good dog wouldn't no one get close to him he was well trained. we even let Smooth get in the wicker chair and take pictures too. Once we went on a family trip to Mississippi to meet our relatives there and daddy wanted us to see where he came from you know where he grew up it took us two day driving in the car to get there but it was a small town and we had to walk a long way to get to the store but you could buy this bologna and it was sweet it was the best bologna I ever ate they had chickens in the yard cow's and two pig's but you didn't mess with the pigs they would bite you. They grew all kinds of stuff and when my great auntie cooked dinner that day she got one of the chickens out the yard snap it's neck took all the feathers off and fried it in grease and made some potatoes with some corn she picked from out in the field behind the house and the best tasting sweet biscuits you would ever eat in your whole life but I couldn't eat that chicken. We would sit out on the porch and listen to daddy and auntie tell old stories of the family and eat on some roasted pecan it would be so dark you couldn't see you own hand in front of your face then they would start scaring you with spooky stories.I had a great great uncle who was born in 1876 and was a full blood Indiana and could do some amazing thing. It sure was strange to me that every body I met in the town was a cousin, aunt or uncle we were kin to every body in that town. Daddy & ma-ma said that's how it is oh well I got a lot of people in Mississippi. When we got back to Chicago I thought to my self people would not believe what we came from. Our family was one of the best self contained unit's in the world we were really together and strong . . . .

Until later years when we were all grown up. The reconstruction of the family, when all the ciaos started. People would believe any thing anyone said about us if you didn't know any better.

It was nothing our parents did they were more than good to us all the direction they gave us was on the money the love they gave us was unconditionally the teaching of God's love right from wrong strongly instill in us. So you have to ask your self what went wrong.

CHAPTER 2

Well in the 1970s things started to happen with the family my big sister Stacy had a baby it was my parents first grand child it was a boy I was so attached to the baby I wanted to keep him all the time so I did when Stacy started to work I would keep the baby after I got out of school but of course ma-ma would later come home from work and she would take over then eventually Stacy moved out back to the west side but in my aunties' basement apartment. I was so attached to my sister I would ride the bus every weekend from the south side to the west side to be with her and the baby. when school was out for the summer brake I would stay for weeks or until I got lonely for the rest of the family I especially like being with my big brother Tommy I was sort of a tom boy and he had lots of friends I could play with wrestle, race on our bikes do flips and play fight I was a tom boy what can I say?

I had two other sisters Sue & Diane but it was cool to be with them but all they wanted to do was play with dolls and for me to take them to the park. it was fun but I rather be with the boy's or my big sister.

About a year later my daddy gave Tommy his first car all of us was excited and I couldn't wait to get in that car with him I knew he was going to drive fast like when he drive his mini bike down the ally I think I was more excited than him like it was my gift oh wow it was a happy day.

I know Tommy was happy if you could have seen the look on his face trying to act like he was cool.

Later that year more black families began to move into the area and that just added to our family which made more mouths for ma-ma to feed because all of us would bring friends home everyday and everybody loves ma-ma cooking even our friends' parents.

I have 5 more brothers we are a beautiful family. As we all get older and find our own individualities 'family life take on a change first Stacy move to a different part of town and has new friends that make a change in the way I am allowed to visit. but I notice a change in her but I couldn't put my finger on it so I went along not knowing what was up but I still love my sister yet I was a little naïve but also young at the time.

Now Stacy was taking pill with her friends. I didn't know what to do if I should tell my mother, father or talk to her and ask her why she was doing this or what I was afraid that something would happen to her I didn't know what to do so I cried the next day I ask her why she was doing it and she said it's nothing but I saw her about a week later at her friends house she was sitting in on the couch and when I walked she could barely lift her head she was so high off pills I rushed over and pushed her head up and called her name she looked at me and said in a calm voice what's wrong with you girl? What's wrong with you I ask? Are you trying to kill yourself or something? Come on get up lets go home. I held her by her arm and we walked down the hall and she assured me she could walk by her self once we were in her house she drank some water and said I got to go to the store I need to go grocery shopping. so we went to the store while shopping I was so worried and watching her I didn't pay any attention to what she was putting in the cart once at the register I helped her to pay for the groceries and when we were back at her house unpacking the groceries that's when I notices we had spent $230.00 on nothing but cookies and one big pack of ground beef. We just laughed while laughing her boyfriend Jeffery walked in he ask what happen. Why are you laughing?

She answered we went to the grocery store all I bought was cookies. It turned out to be a good day after she slept the day away I never saw her like that again if she was still doing the drugs I couldn't tell.

Now my brother Tommy he end up going to jail that was his first time not living at home after a year we would see him everyday because he could come out for work release the jail would let him out to go to work everyday and he had to be back at the jail at a certain time for the night until his jail term was up. He was in jail for selling drugs where he picked that up I don't know.

I use to drop him off every night when it was time for him to return. but when he got out we would go out on the weekend to all the steppers set if it wasn't that we would go to concerts it was so much fun me and Tommy. He would work on cars and was good at it. He still does it to this day.

He met and married this girl down the street and boy did they start having babies! Then things started to slow down we didn't go out to the clubs like we used to and most of the time I could always find him at home. He would always have a friend or two there. His wife start to complain but it was not just because of the company he kept she said I needed to talk with him because he was snorting that stuff, using drugs I was in aw and I just started watching him to see for myself and over time I saw it I really saw it.

I went to his house one day when I was on my way home so I just stopped by he was in the back room sitting in the chair nodding slob running from the side of his mouth and when he looked up at me I ask what the hell is wrong with you ? What you talking about? He replied looking all drugged out. You know what I'm talking about look at you high as hell! All I could see was that time when I found my sister like that it's hard to see someone you love and have spent your whole life looking up to those and wanting to be like them and find them in a positions like that it really hurt and what can you do? At first you tell yourself you can fix it so you try to help them or at lease you think you are helping them but in reality your just end up coddling them giving them money and all they do is go buy drugs you want to tell somebody but you don't want to be a rat. They would rather buy drugs than food and it gets so bad that when you see them coming you want to run and hide. Because you knew they were going to beg for money and it would only get worse from there.

Then as time passes and I really began to grow up now knowing the signs of a drug user it was more than relevant that I had 2 sisters and 3 brothers on drugs. Most of them were using the same drug heroin; some were on cocaine snorting it. Smoking it I don't know what ever they were doing they were using it.

A few months pass a new family has moved in on the south west corner on the end of the block. The family consist of 2 boys and 3 girls I guess they were all sisters & brothers there wasn't a father just the mother

First I met the girl her name was Sally she was my age. the other two were younger than her then Sally introduced me to her brothers one was Earl he was oldest of the family then there was Blaque he was older than me but he was

So fine and I like him so I began talking to him. he was tall dark and handsome and when I say dark I do mean dark but he was fine! We began to date and see each other. Everyday I was still in school and he was in an alternative school. I had one more year to go before I would graduate. Blaque and I only got closer I was in love. I began to spend more & more time with him. His mother was always at work but eventually we met she was a nice lady but now I could see why they were all so tall.

I had practically moved in with him, he had the basement part of the house. Now I got only months before I graduate from high school now I find out I'm pregnant what am I going to do? Nothing. I tried to hide it from my parents and it worked for 6 months and when it was confirmed my daddy and I had a long talk and daddy cried and now he really didn't like Blaque.

I didn't understand why daddy cried but it later made sense to me it was because he was hurt because he had bigger plans for me and my life, daddy was disappointed in me he thought of me as an more goal oriented individual he believed I was the one more likely to succeed he didn't think I would get pregnant at this point in my life. But I still graduated and went to college so it wasn't that bad.

When I had the baby I was in college after my baby was 6mos. Old I went right back to school and got my associate then I was working not in my field but working then I went to school for cosmetology and got licenses for that and I have been doing hair sense. So I did succeed.

Now after a few years Blaque and I aren't together any more but its o-k we are still good friends and God has a way of working things out. what I do is hang around my family pretty much especially when I am not working and I like to go see daddy with his band whenever I can, that's how I met the love of my life.

And I just love him so much he is the best man in the whole wide world but that's another story.

Our family was so tight you couldn't pour water between us we would get together and play in the back yard just play horse shoes tic tack toss and daddy kept us a dog as a pet we as kids didn't want for anything we had bike's, roller skates, ice skates, archery set, mini bike's most of all we had love. Daddy even had two snow mobiles for us and we would go up to the park with daddy and ride. some times daddy would take us up to Wisconsin to ride and you know our friends wanted to go. As we got older we were such a self contain unit we did everything as a unit where one went the other went you know ma-ma kind of raise us like that if one wasn't welcome then nobody was and as we got older that just stuck with us we would have parties in the basement. In the summer time we would get together with our friends in two three carloads of us and take food and a grill and go to the beach my brother Tommy would drive the car daddy gave him and my sister Stacy and her husband would drive the next car, one of our friends from the neighborhood would drive and off we would go. we always did things together ma-ma had no worries when we were all together we were a family.

Once Tommy Stacy and I went out to a party on the west side to a place called MGM Grand it was a real popular place at the time the place was always packed a really nice club the tone was mellow a mixture of people we would dance all night mostly what is called stepping one night Stacy got so drunk we had to walk her to the car with no shoes she didn't walk much better with her shoes off. Then she started to puke up every where next we had to get her something to eat.

So now we are on the way to her house and she had to puke again Tommy had to carry her to her door and we decided to stay the night. The next day Tommy and I teased her but over all it was a fun night. My brother Tommy was a tall young man and he was a little head strong daddy use to tell him not to be driving all his friends around in the car all the time and it was one particular person daddy didn't like or trust Tommy with so daddy told him not to keep driving him around in his car that he wasn't his friend just because he smile and lie to you don't make him your friend but Tommy didn't listen.one night Tommy was driving around with crook in his car yeah you heard me right his name was crook at lease that what everybody called him. I wonder why? He dropped him off and parked the car in front of the house when he went out to his car that morning his car wasn't there some body stole it and you know who it was Tommy's car had a shut off switch on it and the only way you could start it was to turn off the shut off and Tommy told Crook about it like a fool now he don't have a car. Now daddy not wanting to say I told you so he didn't have too. The next day daddy went to work and said for us to stay in the house until ma-ma got home and don't have no company in the house about 30 minutes after daddy left Tommy let his friend in the house he knew better but did it any way. Tommy was in the basement where daddy kept his entire music equipment amps PA system microphone you know stuff he needs for the band. Daddy came back no one was expecting him to come back so soon. Daddy ask when Tommy was I said in the basement daddy went to the basement and he saw that boy and Tommy down there messing with his guitar call their self playing daddy was so mad he just snapped he made the boy get out daddy ask Tommy why did he have him in the house when he told him not to have company Tommy just stood there daddy told him to get up stairs when they got upstairs daddy started to take off his belt Tommy was trying to go to the upstairs and he got smart with daddy. Daddy looked at him in disbelief I don't know why Tommy did that daddy hit Tommy so hard and so fast he knocked him up all the stairs to the up stairs and Tommy was laying there in a fetal position when daddy made him get up and come down the stairs Tommy had blood running out of both his ears. I was crying I was scared I hadn't never seen daddy like that before daddy didn't hit him anymore I think it scared him too. Tommy never did disobey daddy again.

I can remember so many days and nights of good time and the not so good but most of the times were just pure innocent fun spent with my family. One day in August it was so hot we all went swimming even ma-ma it was so hot we were all over the place in and out of the water every time we would dry off we would go back in again ma-ma just sat watching us and laughing at the stupid thing we were doing while keeping her feet in the water then finally it was time to go as we rode home and started to dry off it only got hotter and hotter when we got home ma-ma made us all take a bath and put on some cool clothes she fried some sweet potatoes and fried some chicken made a big jug of tea and before we could eat ma-ma had us to bring two mattresses off the beds and the little TV out the kitchen and put it on the front porch and that's where we all slept.

When it got too hot we would al ways make a palette weather it was in the living room or on the porch it didn't matter but it sure was fun

Things like that you can't do today if you slept on your porch on the south side in Englewood you might not wake up . . .

One year ma-ma gave all the girl born in August Stacy, Sue and me a surprise birthday party in the back yard the back yard was decorated so nice and all our friends and cousins and family were there some of which we hadn't seen in years and they took so many pictures and we were dancing and there was so much food ma-ma had cooked so much food but she didn't make the cake like she normally do from scratch but the cake was so good and it was big it was yellow cake with strawberry and pineapple filling with butter cream frosting and it had all our names on it

That was another beautiful family day ma-ma plan.

When ma-ma started to work for Steward Bus Co. she was a driver and was good at it she would drive the wheels off that bus and ma-ma was able to bring her bus home she kept it all the time I guess it was because she would do late runs sometimes I started to working with her on the bus I was her assistance I would help her load the people that were in wheelchairs and those that weren't I would make sure that they were in seatbelts that was my job ma-ma and I would be allover town on that bus as long as we were on time to pick them up we would go to all the thrift shop up north.

CHAPTER 3

I remember one day we stayed too long and was almost late for our school pick up and ma-ma was driving that bus and when she turned that corner and pulled in the parking spot hell I flew out of my seat and slid all the way to the front of the bus down by her feet and she just laughs and said that's why you suppose to have on your seat belt and ma-ma had tears in her eyes she laughs so hard.

It was a lot of fun working with Ma-ma all the places we would go in the span of a week and ma-ma knew so many people some times we would go to take the people to Ringling Bro. Circus and that was very interesting.

Ma-ma and I would drive all over the city seeing things I didn't know existed. I am so glad I had the opportunity to share this with my mother. I changed jobs but no matter what I was doing or where I was I would still make my way to ma-ma everyday. I completed my license for cosmetology now I can do hair full time and legally in a shop even though I have been doing it all the time. We have been living on the south side for some years now and I must admit it is different from the west side the people for one are much warmer on the west side and it just seem like it more fun but that's just me I still go on the west side I think I will always love the west side.

Now I am a little bit older and I really know my way around town I have my own car and I just go everywhere I try to go to all the places daddy plays when he is performing in the city ma-ma don't come out that much with daddy any more although she use to but every sense she was at a show with daddy on the west side and a man was trying to rob the place and he got killed when the robber was shot in the head his bone flew out his head and right by ma-ma's feet and that stopped her from going. I think that would have stopped me too.

But I go to all of his shows when I leave work I always try to take someone with me so that everybody would know my daddy and how good he is he's just the greatest. Daddy would tell me about the business things I should be aware or because he knew I had stars in my eyes and I could sing by listening to my daddy about the business I decided to go back to school for business that was my major and I did learn a lot by daddy knowing this he would often ask for my knowhow about certain things and have me fill out some papers I became his secretary in so many words. I knew every place daddy would be playing what night of the week and most of the time I would be there and I would become a fixture I met a lot of the blues great like Ko Ko Taylor, Buddy Guy, Hubert Summlin, Guy King just to name a few and they knew me because daddy would all know I was his daughter and his pride.

None of my other brother and sister would go to see daddy they thought it was boring because it was the blues I didn't feel that way I was interested in what my daddy was doing and I could always learn more to help myself. I don't think they knew how great daddy was. Never taking the time to find out showing no interest in him what he was capable of doing what it was that made it possible for him to provide for us. What the people around the world were talking about. I don't know if they cared to know what daddy had become how very famous he is.

A lot of things happen in the course of daddy having his own band daddy would talk to me about it one time daddy wa sin the mix of what to do about his drummer who at the time was Pete and it was hard for him because there was some things that daddy didn't agree on and did not think it was professional or the way he wanted his band to be presented daddy believed in respect of your self and others that was something Pete wasn't showing on a number of occasions he got warning and seem to just ignore them so daddy had to let him go.

Daddy asks me did I know this guy named Dave.

I do a lot of hair on 63rd & Ashland and I know a lot of people I did know him and his girl the lady that worked with me knew him real well but I did know him so when daddy ask me did I think that he would fit his band I said yeah he could work so daddy and I talked some more about Dave and my advice to daddy was to give him a try if he wasn't pleased he could always find some one else. That's what daddy did.

Now he had a new drummer and a friend and Dave worked out with daddy until daddy passed daddy would always ask me for advice if I thought I could help I would give it to him but one thing I would do in a heartbeat is if I didn't know I would tell him right quick I don't know rather than to give him bad advice but most of the time daddy had his mine already made up about what he was going to do I think he just like to keep me involved or make me feel like a part of his life.

Life was good my sister Stacy was doing fine she had start doing hair I was honored when she ask me what I thought if she should do hair or not and I told her yes why not? And she did now there are two stylists in the family then my other sister

Sue went to hair school with Stacy. You think I encouraged that? Nope or maybe any way it was good now we were all doing something positive and ma-ma &daddy could be proud of their tribe.

Stacy & Sue were in school for hair my brother Tommy was fixing cars, Will was working at Montgomery ward auto dept David was doing contractor work on homes I was still doing hair on Ashland all that wasn't working were in school

The family remained strong. That summer one hot day ma-ma & I, Sue were sitting on the porch just enjoying The weather Stacy had only left by minutes when we got a call telling us that her husband Jeffery of 17 yr had just got kill within minutes her kids came and we had to brake the news to them that wasn't easy now we had to get the car and try to find Stacy to inform her of what happen we didn't find her until late at night and she had already heard the news so I went with her to the hospital my heart just cried for her after that we couldn't find her for days we needed her to take care of arrangements but when she was found Jeffery's mother had done every thing. what was so bogus was that they didn't even put her name on the obituary and that really hurt her we were under the impression that his family loved her for all of those years but death brings about a change in people at this time Stacy started doing drugs really bad and no matter what we tried it just didn't help maybe that was her way of dealing with his death her escape from the reality this went on for years Stacy didn't do hair in the shop any more she couldn't because of her drug habit. She did it as a hustle a way to get drugs she would go to people's house and do their hair for $20.00. I would tell her to come to the shop and help me be my shampoo girl from Thursday thru Saturday and when the booster came in selling thing I would always buy things for her and myself and I would take her with me to the clubs on the weekend so I knew she wasn't getting high for that time cause I would pin her to my side and buy her all the drinks (which was mostly beer) she wanted I would rather see her a little tipsy from that than high off drugs I did it as long as I could about a year or something later it could be more she moved to Rockford IL.

I would talk to her often. I had not seen her face to face for about 8 months she had told me that she had kicked the drugs and was doing fine. Her kids would come to the city so I had heard that she was on something called a meth program and trying to get her life together. I thought that was excellent time had passed. One day while working at the shop some one had ask me about the girl that use to shampoo for me I said that was my sister and she had moved to Rockford and was doing fine so now all day I kept on thinking about Stacy. the next day which was a Saturday once I finished working I jumped in my car went by ma-ma's house and let her know I was going up to Beloit to see Sophia and while I was there I was going to see Stacy. I had this strong yearning to see Stacy I wanted my sister so when I got to Sophia's house I sat with everyone for a short then I told Sophia to show me where Stacy lived Rockford was only a 15 minuet drive on the back road from Beloit WI so we took that ride I didn't know where Stacy lived because I had never been there before when we got to Stacy's house there was no one there. Sophia and I left I said we would come back in the morning and try again. we went back to Sophia's house had a few beers and talked for a few hours then we went to bed once we woke up that morning took a shower ate a little and headed to Stacy's house again still no luck I went there for a week and didn't get no one I had to go back home and work so I left and headed back to the city when I got to Chicago the first thing I did was go to my mothers house and let her know I didn't find Stacy or her kids we talked for a short time then I went home got a shower and went to the shop I had a few clients waiting on me when I got there then about and hour later here comes my niece Stacy's daughter I looked at her and said girl it sure is hard to find you all I been to your house for a week straight while I was at Sophia's house and I didn't get nobody ask Sophia she'll tell you how many times we went to you house man. She said that's because don't nobody live there anymore we moved and we live at bob's sister house. what? Who the hell is bob? That's my ma-ma new boyfriend said my niece when all this happen I ask. Auntie that old news ma-ma is here now call granny shell tell you. That's just what I did and ma-ma told me that Stacy was just here(ma-ma was working at the corner store at the time) she just went down to the house call the house she's there so I did when Stacy got on the phone I was trying to tell her that I was just at her house looking for her and I had just got back then all of a sudden I hear a lot of commotion in the back round then my brother was on the phone then I was talking to my other sister Sue it seem like they were tell Stacy not to go somewhere something was going on I didn't understand what was happening so I just hung up the phone. I rushed to get my other clients shampooed and under the dryer and I ask the other stylist to keep an eye on them to I got back and told them I would be right back I had to run to my mothers house for a minuet it was important when I got there I had just missed her I just shouted out dame I keep missing her but Tommy explain to me what all the commotion was Stacy was talking about going to Mississippi where she was going to get her 3 acres left to her from her husband Jeffery and make a new start and every one there was telling her not to go.

I went back to the shop so I could finish my work. when I got done with my regular clients I did my niece hair once I was done with her I was done for the day so I clean my station and me and my niece went to the store and I bought some beer and went to ma-ma's house. I sat on the porch drank a couple of beer talk with ma-ma and my brother then I went home I was tired after this whole day once I got home I took another shower to wash all that hair off me and the dirt from the day and went to my bedroom turn the TV on and started to watch a movie and I was sleep. The telephone rings it's my mother and I knew something was wrong she was upset but tried to keep her composer and told me that Stacy was in the hospital she had an asthma attack and the doctor said it didn't look good. I didn't ask any questions I just told ma-ma I'm on my way and hung up the phone before I could get fully dress the phone rang again it was my baby sister she was crying and said your sister is dead and I just drop the phone I was overwhelm . . .

When I got to ma-ma house I found out she was on her way to get her land with that man Bob and while they were on the high way she had asthma attack and her pump was broke she was in Fort Wayne IN. the story didn't sit right with me I know Stacy and she wouldn't had a broke asthma pump and on the highway isn't no way Stacy would not have checked her pump long before that it isn't right something else happen but never the less I'm less one sister. Now daddy, ma-ma and I take that long solemn drive to find my sister and get her car and property and look thru her belonging to see if we could find her insurance papers we never did find any but her daughter swear she had some with her and Bob don't know what we were talking about at less that's what he said. As daddy would say it is what it is . . . .

I had search for my sister a whole week and when I finally catch up to her she was dead you know that hurt me deep
Now I know why I needed to see her.

I know that took a piece of daddy's heart he was so hurt he didn't know how to grieve for Stacy and be strong for ma-ma she was lost too.
I did all I could financially and when it was all over I had taken Stacy's kids in to live with me. God had bless me with a 4

bedroom house with a den I had more than enough room so I took them in Stacy had 4 kid only 3 live with me and that was the girls the oldest boy stayed with ma-ma. It was hard

Having her kids with me didn't make it any easier for me but I made it thru after 2 yrs her girls came of age and decided to move out on their own I didn't stop them but let the find their own they wouldn't be with me for ever so it was relevant that they find their own way plus one of the girls were pregnant they had money from their parents. I just made them promise to me that they would keep in touch with me and let me know where they were and keep me with good contact information on their where a bouts nothing else. That what they did

After that the family tried to find a place of normalcy and continue to move forth. It took a while we found something to flue us and we kept on going. As time pass on the years seem to pass rapidly. Some of my brothers were in jail and other were still lost in their drug world but some how you seem to keep loving and caring for them and it's still a family maybe a dysfunctional but my family. If you don't have family something you have become accustom to having you are lost if you ever admit it or not be it what it may you can always pick your friends but you can't pick your family.

My life hasn't been all roses but I think it has been pretty good with all my up and downs and turn a rounds now comes the time where my test in life has comes.

In November of 2005 daddy began to complaint about getting sick all the time he believed he had asthma I listen to him but in my mind I believed it to be something different but I didn't know. But what I did do is observe him by me being around him all the time next I began to talk to my mother about how she thought daddy was doing. Ma-ma said she thought daddy was doing fine but on one occasion daddy had woke one morning and said to her look while point to his underpants and there was blood she said it was not a lot but still enough to alarm you especially when he said all he had done was pass gas. I didn't ask daddy about it but with me that set of a red flag so now I am really watching him

One night while at the club during one of his show daddy got sick and couldn't play anymore this so my husband and I had to take him to the hospital.

We had the Dr. check daddy for everything and he said was bothering him daddy was fine and he was just stressed out that was just because daddy kept telling the doctor he had asthma and he didn't look daddy was 69 years old and never had asthma in his life his mother did my mother did I have sister and brothers that have it but daddy never did.

But the doctor gave him a new asthma medicine to take and we went home with a appointment in hand a few months passed and things looked o-k daddy had to go to the University of Illinois once a month for his check up sense his heart attack in 1985 but it seemed as thought everything was fine because the doctors there never did mention anything to him about cancer. One week after that we had to rush daddy to the hospital he stayed there for three days that's when we found out daddy was really sick! This really tore a hole in my heart. A father is a girls first love and a boys hero to me my daddy was both I couldn't imagine the thought of losing him daddy being gone for about three years now not here to talk over major decision with me not taking pictures in the wicker chair not telling stories of the family. No more daddy, Guy and I at his shows. Nothing? But my daddy the strong man that he was . . . is still strong I feel him around me everyday giving me that extra push when needed. He's still strong

CHAPTER 4

Daddy was still doing his gigs every night and didn't seem to be that sick and then again one night in February he had to be rushed to the hospital he wasn't breathing real well and he couldn't control his bowels so he had to stay in the hospital until the doctor could get it under control before he left the hospital most of the time my mom my husband and I were always there at the hospital with daddy and he knew he was coming to the end and he would tell us what he wanted us to do. Daddy would have visit from fellow musicians most of the time it was ma-ma Guy and me daddy would do a lot of talking and sometime throw in a joke or two he still had a sense of humor before he was released from the hospital he was put on chemo and had a pod inserted to his chest.

Daddy continued to make his gigs on about the 15th of February daddy just couldn't go no more. One week and a half later was daddy's birthday he made 70 years old February 24th 2006

On March 3rd 2006 daddy went to heaven.

It was a sad day for the whole family especially Ma-ma not to mention that daddy was all she had known he was her life 50 years of marriage at this point I have to be strong for ma-ma and that in turns means the responsibility of everything fall on me. Not to even seem like I am complaining God knows that I am not I am more that happy to be here to do whatever I can to help my mother and father its' more than a pleasure it's a privilege it's a blessing that a person can have a child that in their heart they know they can depend and never worry about things not being taken care of. You know what I didn't know that my parent's thought that much of me especially my mother I was kind of blown away when I came to realize that she had put so much love and trust in me. I know she would come to me and ask my opinion about things when I started to here from her best friend, people from our church friends in the neighborhood of how she trust me how she was proud of me.

I could only smile because I just wasn't aware

Ma-ma and I didn't always get alone when I was younger from about the age of 15 thru 20 yrs. Ma-ma said I was head strong and my mouth was going to get me kill I talked to much I had to speak my mind I didn't believe in holding anything back if it came up in my mind then you can believe it came out. And I didn't much care who it was with the exception of my parents I kind of toned it you know rephrased it but I had to say what I felt. I got a lot of ass whipping too you better believe that once I moved out of the house thing began to change wit ma-ma and I they got much better. I was able to talk to her with out her shouting at me. and I learned how to deal with thing from a different level if things started to get ugly I would just say ma-ma I am going to go now I will call you later. I would go home so I wouldn't say something I would later regret.

Ma-ma would tell me how much of a woman I had become her friends had great admiration for me and would tell ma-ma you should be proud of her she's' going to be somebody you raised her right and ask if I was the oldest child ma-ma would tell them no and Ruby would be surprised and say she act so mature she such a little lady. Like I said thing only got better and better with ma-ma and me. Ma-ma was and will always be the lady of my life my queen. For her and daddy to believe in me enough to choose me

To be the responsible one to oversee all the business to along with my mother not to mention the entire bill paying before hand getting daddy back and forth to the hospital to be his care giver and when I wasn't there it was on ma-ma and we did everything we could to make thing comfortable for him until that time. Before daddy passed he sat and talked with me, ma-ma and my husband and gave extensive direction on what he wanted done with certain things and who he didn't want to have anything. Daddy left almost everything to my mother, me and a few things he left to my husband. My brothers didn't like that but daddy word is his bond and that's how it have always been there were several things like the house, car's musical equipment jewelry, royalties from record companies. Other odds that only ma-ma and I have exclusive right. And my brother's and sisters are aware of this not saying that they like it but they know it and it became more relevant when I moved my away.

The family was crazy leaching all over my mother as if they could con her out of things. When it came down to it and ma-ma would tell them to talk to me they didn't like it not one bit everything was passed to my mother and me. If there was a decision and ma-ma wasn't sure with her decision before hand she would ask me I would tell her if that is what she wanted to do whatever you want to do ma-ma. But I would think to myself about the times when ma-ma and daddy couldn't put anything down and would be on edge when company come over because things would just come up missing all of them we're stealing from ma-am, daddy whoever it didn't matter to them as long as they could buy drugs they stole so much from my parent's it was a shame I mean money, clothes, jewelry, food out the freezer, DVD, if it wasn't nail down you can forget it cause somebody got it. and they didn't have decency enough to try to help pay a bill or buy grocery but my lil sister Diane would buy food for her and her kids not enough to last the month because she had to have some of her food stamps to sell and you didn't get dollar for dollar so you could sell $100.00 for $65.00

It got so bad that ma-ma and daddy had to lock up their bedroom and any thing they wanted they had to put it inside that include food you know certain the deep freezer had a lock on it ma-ma kept the key on her car keys and the freezer locked then one day somebody broke the lock off their bedroom door and stole ma-ma's leather coat and some jewelry.

It was really bad my parents were so hurt that they had raised all these children and given them a good start in life all the tools they would need to be successful and most of them are on drugs and I know that took a chunk out of them because they told me and often embarrassed to them. but like I would tell them it's nothing you done it's just the choice they made not a good one but still their own choice they grown and has been for a long time what can you do?

Now the worst thing I seen was when daddy was coming to the end lying in that bed and I had to give him his medicine when I went to give him his dose I notice that the pills had been tampered with so I called ma-ma and showed her the pills and ask her did she do this because the pills had been punched out and there was a poor attempt to recover them

Now I look at the pills closely as I push it out and it's not the right pill so I check and about 6 of the original pills were substituted with something different isn't that a bitch! Now I go to get his bottle of morphine and I can't find it. It just simply disappears. what if I wasn't paying attention I could have gave daddy the wrong medicine and kill him it's a crying shame someone would steel a dying man's medication just to fed their addiction now I have to call the doctor to get more medicine for my daddy wont be in pain it's worst that embarrassing and they have nerve to ask about what was left for them . . . should it be? Daddy knew what he was doing by leaving things to ma-ma and me after daddy died things started coming up missing not like it wasn't before his death but this was ridiculous a couple of his guitars came up mission a lot of his and ma-ma jewelry, cloths, and his gold tooth things continued to disappear I had to check on my mother everyday hell they might have stole her.

I would take her shopping to try to make her feel better it didn't work but I did it anyway I know all she wanted was daddy back but I couldn't do that I would do any thing I could for my mother sometimes I would fix her hair arch her eyebrows take her out to eat spend the whole day with her help to pay the bills what ever ma-ma wanted some days we would sit and talk all-day about daddy the family and how hurt she was about them being all fucked up on drugs and out of all of her children it was only one she could confide in and trust that has got to hurt after raising 10 to what you consider your best and come up with 1,that has got to make you feel like you failed as a mom but I lived the life with her and I know better she could never fail as a good mother or a person not just by man but by God ma was good but this took a lot out of ma-ma we didn't use to be like that.

What do you do? You don't just stop loving some one just because they mad a bad choice and it's not like you can turn off real love someone you've known and had all your life. Now with daddy gone his death has really taken a toll on Ma-ma I had to go and pick up my lil sister from the bus station on 95th when I got there I drove pass her 3 times then I called ma-ma to make sure I was at the right place because I didn't see her or her kids then ma-ma told me yeah you at the right place hold on let me call her. she click over and called Diane then ma-ma click back to me and said drive thru there again she is going to be standing out in front ok ma-ma I said when I drove around she ran out in front of my car and scared the hell out of me I didn't know who she was she looked so bad I thought she was one of those homeless hypes I didn't know that was my sister.

I get out helping her and the kids put their stuff in the car all the time I'm trying not to stare at her. Then I start the conversation by asking her so girl how you doing? She looks at me and says its so sad daddy gone. She start something that I think was suppose to be crying there were some tears but it stopped as fast as it started everybody grieve differently.

Diane tells me I am not going to stay at ma-ma's for a long time it's just for a little while she said. Well that's between you and ma-ma I don't have nothing to do with it I said. When we got to the house she went in with the girls and just forgot all about her stuff or thought I was going to take it inside for her wrong!! Hey I shouted out to her you forgot your stuff you better get it if you want it. I'm not going to carry it for you. She told the kids to get it and then she went in the house grab ma-ma and cried some more after talking for a while she told ma-ma the same thing she told me she wasn't going to be there long.

That soon turned in to months and that turned into a year now ma-ma has been taking care of her and her kids all this time like it's her obligation and Diane has 6 kids and don't take care of them. ma-ma does it for her. now Diane runs off to Iowa and leave her kids on ma-ma and my brother Will is there with his woman look it s about 11 people living in the house and no one is paying any bills but ma-ma & me when she tells me something is due and she don't have the money.

They are just killing my mother with all this shit Diane kids go to jail then call my ma-ma to get them out the other wants shoes and think my ma-ma should buy them but they don't ask their ma-ma Diane all the time stuff still coming up missing money out of her purse every thing ma-ma sleeps on her purse what kind of shit is that? Everyday it some kind of confusion Will want to get high worrying ma-ma Diane kids with their friends all over the house smoking refer and lying about that and Diane come back when she wants to like she don't even have kids then she wants to fuss like somebody owes here something.

I don't want my mother to get sick she has asthma and that's enough but if I let it go they going to kill my ma-ma so now I come up with a plan Sophia now lives in Arizona and I have been there about 4 times and I keep trying to get ma-ma to go Sophia has been there for about 4 years with her brother and her kids so I talk ma-ma into going I paid for her ticket and send her there for 2 weeks she likes it and I also know that Arizona is good for her asthma.

Ma-ma talked about it for week how much fun she had and how much she enjoyed it so the next time she went I paid for her to get there and Sophia paid for her to fly back ma-ma couldn't stop talking about how she enjoyed it and that when she is there she don't get sick with asthma so now I am trying to convince her to move there she wont be by herself and she do have family there plus she wont be under all the stress for other people kids, worrisome ass drug users and not worry about the mortgage on the house even though it's not much like about a year and a half to go before it all done.

She is leaning the right way and I know ma-ma is tried I can see it in her face she is lonely for my daddy and don't want to be bothered with those grown ass sister and brother with all their issues. I had to let my shop go because I needed to help them and with all the stress family and business something had to go and I knew what took presence over my salon and it was Ma-ma &Daddy if god give it once he will surly give it again the second will be in more abundance I will trust in god and do what I did walk away.

Now comes the third time and ma-ma's on her way to Arizona again

I told Sophia when ma-ma get there this time to take her around to places so she could find her somewhere to move something that she would be happy with and affordable make sure its' close to where you lives, once you find something let me know. When ma-ma arrived the first thing she did was take a shower and got something to eat and off to the stores ma-ma loved to shop we talked every hour on the hour just so I could get up dates on how ma-ma was and what she was doing you know just to see how she was enjoying herself and if she really wanted to move there. I know it was a lot of memories in that old house mostly good. The time she shared with daddy, watching us grow into adulthood. The times watching and counting all of the grand children born in that house. the later years has taken a toll the heart ship of watching her children deteriorate before here very eyes looking at the seeds of seeds from her that were just out Landis and disrespectful and finally the lost of daddy I think that was it. She was ready to take the challenge to make a change.

I believed she was ready I just wanted to make sure.

About 3 days before ma-ma was due to come home she called me and told me she had found her a place a nice place she was so happy ma-ma went on to describe the place and told me she had to pay a deposit, how much she had with her and what she would need.

CHAPTER 5

I am so convinced that ma-ma want to move I ask ma-ma are you sure? Are you ready to make that move it's a long way from Chicago you know the only other you have ever lived was in Mississippi before you move to Chicago and this is the only place you know as home. It will be a while before I can move there I won't come when you go it will be at lease 10 months before I move there I will be there to visit you in 1 month I said. Child ma-ma said I know you will but its' all right you will have to take care of the house and everything you know you got to sell it if you aren't going to live there. I know I can count on you to do things. now I can get away from all those other dame fools I know I don't have to worry with all their bullshit I am going to be too far for them to come and bother me and I got a place that big enough for me I can make room for somebody to stay with me if I want to but I don't want nobody living with me not any of them that what I am trying to get away from now your daddy isn't there now what I need to stay there for? To watch over some grown fools who don't listen yeah I'm ready baby ma-ma said. Do you know when I am coming back? Ma-ma asks yes. You will be back on Tuesday right I said yeah that's right ma-ma said

What are you going to do about the house?

Do you like it?

Yes ma-ma said.

What do you need me to do? I ask

Well ma-ma I think if you like the place and want to get it I think you should pay your security deposit now or at lease before you leave that a way when you move there you can move right in your own house. I still have your money do you need it? Do you want me to send it to you? Tell me what you want me to do. I ask

Well just send me $400.00 and I will go and pay the security on the place I still have most of the money I left with she said O-k ma-ma I will go to the western union and send you the money as soon as I hang up the phone. You want me to hold on to the rest of the money? I ask. Just hold on to it I trust you. I will call you back later Sophia and I are going to go back over to the house I'll let you know what happen when I call you later. o-k she said

I went and sent the money to her.

When ma-ma came home from the airport I went to pick her up she seemed so happy and began to tell me all about her trip and her new house and how much she liked it I was more happy for her than she was for her self. Right away ma-ma went right into business mode she had everything all planed out in her mind and she knew what she was going to do she started telling me what she had plan to take with her what she was going to sell and what she was going to leave ma-ma had her mind made up and ready to go ma-ma was determined and I was happy about that today is the 28 th of August and ma-ma said that she move in on the 11 th of September that leaves of a little less than two weeks to get things done not to mention I have to drive all the way there

Now for a week and a half I go to the house and help ma-ma to start packing and throw away things and have all the other stuff out side for a yard sell every day until everything is sold now earlier in the week ma-ma and I sold the van then she sold the other car to my niece the only car left is the caddy ma-ma had come up with a plan for what to do with the car she give it to me because we cant find a trailer hitch big enough for the caddy so I take the car now I have three cars to take care of but I told ma-ma I would figure out a way to get the car to her ma-ma is so use to driving herself and not waiting on some one to do thing for her and I don't want her to be so far with out her own I want to give the car back to her and I will. Now Sophia is schedule to have surgery on the same day that ma-ma is suppose to move in at 7: am so now I have to get the time we leave here and how long it will take us to get to Arizona also facture in all the stop's we will have to make and be there on time for Sophia's surgery now I have to get a U-haul and load the hitch now when Ma-ma and I go and get the U-haul hitch go back to the house start to load it I told her to sit down and I would do it ma-ma don't need to be doing all that heavy lifting with my brother there. He just sat there like he wasn't going to do shit Didn't anyone help but that didn't stop me then two of my nephews and one of their friends started to help when they came up and saw me moving all this stuff by myself then it started to rain. When my brothers heard me say to my nephews that I would give them something for helping me now all of a sudden he starts to picking up stuff moving real fast. I know it's only because he wants' some money. I didn't say a word I just let him help finally at about 2: oclock in the morning we had finished. I went and bought some fish from J&J so ma-ma could eat she loved fish any way and J&J was the only thing open so I got enough so everyone could eat and we all just sat around eating and reminiscing it turned out to be a really nice night then I went home it was 4: oclock in the morning and we were planning to leave at 11: oclock in the morning so when I got home my husband was waiting for me he ask me where is the truck?

Right there I said. While pointing across the street

He looked and said angrily

What? Where you going with that? That isn't big enough and it isn't safe you aren't moving nobody with that you must be a dame fool if you think I am going to let you drive all that way like that and with your mother ? What's wrong with you baby? Why aren't you thinking you don't have any sense?

He was so mad at me I didn't know what to do but he was right I had a lot of ma-ma's things inside of the van and when I looked out the window at the van it was kind of dipped in the middle where it was hitched together I Hadn't paid attention and I am glad I have a husband who loves me and did pay attention to every detail if I had drove like that I don't think we would have made it.

Now the next morning I had to get up and go get a truck the right size or he wasn't going to let us leave. so I call ma-ma and told her that she had to come and meet me at the U-haul place on Fullerton & Damen because if I didn't change the truck Guy said he wasn't letting us go because it was to dangerous that if we drove this truck we could turn over the weight of the hitch would pull us over.

I ask her to bring a couple of the boys from the house to help unload and transfer the stuff from one truck to another once she got there I was ready to go the boys and I went right into action it took us about 50 minutes to get it together and we did it now we have to figure out how to get them back to the south side because the car stayed with me and I need to put my van up too.

I decided that all us could fit in the truck and I would drive them back to the house and ma-ma and I would get on the highway from there. That's what I did just before we got on the high way I stopped at the gas station across the way from the highway and ma-ma and I got some snacks and ice, water then I filled up the truck and we were on our way it was rush hour but traffic wasn't that bad ma-ma and I talked and laughed until she fell asleep I drove from about 5:30pm until 6:40 the following morning I just couldn't drive any more I was tired so I pulled over on the sided of the road in-between two 18 wheelers and tried to take a nap I tossed and turned for about 40 minutes and then I told ma-ma I was going to drive some more because I couldn't get comfortable so I couldn't sleep. O-k baby but are you sure? Ma-ma asks.

Yeah I'm sure ma-ma I wouldn't drive if I thought that I couldn't do it and besides I'm not going to put you in danger let only myself. Ok were on the road again put your seat belt on. I said.

I had to drive most of the way although ma-ma could drive and was one of the best drivers I didn't let her drive much because ma-ma couldn't see that good driving at night especially on the highway.

Now I drive and we just boogieing on down the high way and having a good time enjoying the sites and enjoying each others company and the conversation just got better and better.

Ma-ma shared some deep though about her feeling daddy, my sister and brother.

Ma-ma was really hurt about losing daddy she said that he was her life she had been with daddy since she was 17 years old then she started having us but everything she did wanted to do she always confided in daddy she felt so lost without him. now she was going to make a new start at life trying to heal ma-ma was a strong lady when she made her mind up that was it no ifs' ands' or butts' about it. I admire that about her

Ma-am didn't like the fact that my sisters and brothers were using drugs she didn't understand where it all started or came from why were they like that and felt like she fail as a mother but I told her it's nothing you done it's their own choices and when they get tired they will stop lets hope and pry that it's not to late you cant make a grown person do nothing you tell them what you think offer you assistance and prey for them but you cant make them do nothing. ma-ma had not failed as a mother between her and daddy we didn't want for anything most of all not at loving us or giving us attention you know some of us need that more than others. but ma-ma would do special things all the time for us she didn't forget a birthday Christmas nothing she was always thinking about her family.

I know when daddy died ma-ma just got tired of the whole thing you think that that would be a wake up call for them but no it wasn't it look like they just got worst I guess the thought that since daddy was gone they could take advantage of ma-ma play on her take her love as weakness she tried for a year and nine months after daddy died and I guess that was enough the stealing and the lying only got worse now ma-ma was locking up not only her room but now it was food and other things but I will leave it at that.

Ma-ma said it would be easy for her now and she didn't have to take care of nobody but her own body she was right she wanted all that burden off her so she could start to heal on our second day of the drive we cried some but for the most part we laugh a lot it was real cool!! As the night starts to fall I tell ma-ma we need to stop at a motel tonight so we can get some real sleep I will pay for it you don't need to pay and then we can take a bath shower something my panties feel all moist I need to wash it bad ma-ma just laughed at me but I did need to wash the cat cant be all moist and smelly.

At about 8:30 that night we stopped at a motel 6 got a room and when we went to the room it was all stinky I don't know what that smell was but I know my mother and I aren't going to sleep in that so I went back down to the desk and ask the lady what could she do about the room could she give us a better room she was nice about it she gave us a upgrade so now ma-ma and I go to the new room and it was nice we got some things from the truck and a few snack and it was on ! Now I turn on the TV. And guess what? We are traveling right thru three different hurricanes that are all thru Texas so now I am a little worried but not too I know God is with us and I believe he wanted this for ma-ma more than she wants' it for herself. Now ma-ma takes a shower them me we then lay across the bed to watch TV. But before you know it the TV was watching us

I woke up at 5:20 am I went to the bathroom and wash my face brush my teeth and then woke ma-ma up so we could start out once we had gotten dressed we gathered all our belongings and headed out when we reached the lobby there was tea, coffee, fresh fruit, cereal and donuts ma-ma and I got some coffee for the road and off we went it was about 6: o'clock when we hit the highway now were riding really good and making good time it looks as if we were either riding a little ahead of the hurricane or behind it be cause all the bad weather we were hitting was rain at one point it was so bad I thought of pulling off the road until it had passed but I didn't the rain lighted up a little better than it was at lease now I can see and I am not so scared now so I just kept on driving

A few hours pass and ma-ma fell asleep. I think I am doing pretty good I have never drove this far before the most I have ever drove on a road trip was once to New York and my husband did most of the driving. When I went to Memphis I drove all the way there and back but this is a long drive but its ok I only did it because mama ask me. She has so much trust in me. I will do any thing my mother ask me too just because its' ma-ma now don't get me wrong I am not saying like I am perfect or something like that sometimes ma-ma might ask me to do something and I might not want to do it or its' just at the wrong time but I will do it any way just because it's ma-ma

Now at lease 4 hours has passed while ma-ma has been sleeping now she wakes up looking all around but once she saw where we were she was hollering I didn't know what was wrong ma-ma duck down in her seat and called my name and had both her hands over her face I didn't know what the hell was going on.

Ma-ma, ma-ma what's wrong? I ask ma-ma peered a little from between her fingers out the window then over to me but she didn't say anything so I ask again
What's wrong ma-ma?
Girl I am scared I don't like being up on these mountains she said.
Well ok I didn't know what was wrong you had me scared this will be over soon look at the road see how it is leveling out?
If you that scared don't keep looking out the window over the side ma-ma I said. After a few more hours we came to the boarder of New Mexico once we hit the border it's just a long ride it's really nothing to see other than a lot of cactus Oh yeah we saw this huge bird or something like a bird I don't know what the hell it was but it was sitting on top of a mountain and it

looked like its' eyes had light or something anyway I told ma-ma to look at it and she was like what the hell is that?

I don't know we out here in the dark driving and know the aliens are going to get us I said.

What I say that for ma-ma was on the floor laughing so hard when she looked up she had tears in her eyes when she finally got a breath she called me crazy.

CHAPTER 6

I was serious I was scared you know you see all that stuff on TV and it always happen when you are alone on the road in the middle of nowhere

The truth is out there!

Now I am driving a little bit faster

I want to hurry up and get there and besides we have to be there by 7: am Friday because that's when Sophia has surgery

I think we will be there on time I've been driving my but off

Look we left Chicago at 5 something in the evening on Tuesday on Wednesday night we slept at a motel in Texas and on Thursday evening were going thru New Mexico that's good time.

While riding thru Mexico there is light rain but it soon stops as we come up on Tucson AZ ma-ma wanted to stop.

We came upon a place with a few restaurant's and gas stations and a lot of truckers.

I parked the truck and we went into the KFC and had something to eat while sitting and eating the trucker ask

Do you mind if I sit and eat with you ladies?

Ma-ma looked at me as if to ask me if it was ok I didn't care if he sat or not it's not like he was buying our meal.

Yes I said

Have a seat over there ma-ma said and I sat next to her.

As we talked ma-ma ask

How long have you been driving trucks?

I've been driving for about 20 years he said.

Well I bet you know your way all over the place. Ma-ma said

Yeah pretty much. Where are you going? He ask

My daughter and I we're going to phoenix Arizona. Ma-ma said

Well you should be there by 10; o'clock in the morning you're not that far you're just about in Tucson now. He said

Do you know a way were we don't have to go up in those dame mountains? I am so afraid of them. Ma-ma said. You are going to pass though some mountains but the ones you are going to see aren't as bad as the ones you already pass though and it is really no way around it but once you get a little bit father it is going to be a straight shot.

I guess it will be ok and thank you. Ma-ma said

Ma-ma and I left the man sitting there we went to used the washroom then back in the truck and started on our way now I was kind of worried that we wouldn't be there on time for Sophia's surgery but I was going to drive like wind to make it on time . . .

I didn't want her to go into surgery worrying about us or if we were going to be there for her.

Now we are just driving down the highway trying to get to our destination and really just enjoying the sights and it is really a nice serine yet calming drive.

The mountains are beautiful it has just enough color with cactus and all the greenery that just runs all along the sides of the roads. The cactus all take on their own personal shapes like each one has a personality that fits its shape the sky is as clear as the warmth from the sun warms your whole body while the joy and love from Ma-ma and me just fills the truck it's simply beautiful. It's like this trip was ordain from God like it was suppose to be just ma-ma and me . . .

I haven't seen ma-ma so relaxed in along time she's so happy.

It makes my heart happy to see all the smiles on her face I feel like I have done a great service for ma-ma.

Now as we continue to drive the conversation began to slow as ma-ma began to fall asleep and I just keep on driving I feel that we will be there soon then I will go to the hospital and someone will be there to drive ma-ma the rest of the way to her new house and she can get a little bit settled and get some rest she needs it she has been on the road for nearly 3 days and ma-ma's not use to this and she's not twenty five any more she need's to rest and there is still a lot of unpacking to do.

As the dawn began to show I am just coming into a town I just keep on driving and looking as I drive along things start to look a little familiar to me then I notice a sign we are 25 miles from Phoenix ma-ma is sleeping and I don't want to wake her until we are there.

Now I call Sophia's' phone and her husband answered
Hello?
Hello Wayne I said
Who is this? He ask
It's me Jean you know your mother in-law.
Oh he said (with a slight chuckle) I didn't recognize your voice He said.
Where ya'll at? He ask

We're here I call to ask you how do I get to the hospital from here? I said

I am on the expressway coming up to 7th Ave.

Ok get off on 21st Ave make a right and keep straight and you will run right into the hospital you can't miss it the hospital is called Maricopa County medical you know where we came and you talked to the doctor.

Oh yeah I remember I'll call you when I get there I said.

Once I made it to the hospital I didn't have to call him there he was walking out the door just as I pulled up then I saw his mother and his aunt penny too. I got out of the truck ma-ma was woke she had been for a while she got out too and we were hugging and kissing each other you know showing some love so we all go inside to Sophia's room we had just a little time before they took her to the operating room.

She was happy to see us but she had been prep for her surgery already she wasn't feeling no pain right about now.

When the doctor came in I spoke with him for a few minutes and then they took Sophia off to surgery.

At this point we all went out side and worked out a plan of who would do what. Wayne and I stayed at the hospital With Sophia Wayne's Aunt Penny who knew ma-ma would drive her to her house and his mother would go back to the house with Sophia's kids.

Now before arriving at ma-ma's house Penny called her kid's and husband to meet her there and help ma-ma unload the truck.

Once that was done and ma-ma got herself cleaned up she and Penny came back to the hospital to see how Sophia was doing. She was well as to be expected after major surgery it was successful the doctor said that the surgery was the cure. So that was good to here to know that she didn't have to have chemo that's wonderful.

Now when we made it to the hospital it was at 7:05 am that was like 3 hours earlier than the man had said. Now I stay at the hospital all day I even spend the night so when the nurse came in I ask her for a toothbrush My mouth taste like the inside of a sneaker and I cant take it. She was nice about it and then she brought me some blankets and I sleep next to Sophia's bed in two chairs the next day at about noon I left the hospital and went to ma-ma's house and help her with whatever and after wards I took a shower and it felt so nice

Ma-ma and I sat around and talked for a while and ma-ma cooked us breakfast we ate then we went back to the hospital ma-ma still was driving the U-haul she hadn't turned it in.

She was crazy she said it was her car she wasn't going to turn it in until the last minute because she had giving me the car

Ma-ma was running around buying stuff she wanted for her house and just putting it in the U-haul she said she didn't need any body to move nothing for her not as long as she had that truck.

Once we left the hospital we went to Sophia's house and spent some time there with her kids we stayed most of the day that night we went back to the hospital and I told Sophia I had to go back home in the morning my flight leave at 10:45 and I wouldn't be back to the hospital before I left.

Sophia said that she could go home in the morning the doctor told her. I said ok and call my airline and got my departure time changed to tomorrow evening at 5:45 pm so I was there at her house when she came home. Before she came home I went back to ma-ma's house and stayed the night with her.

The bed was up and we sleep like two tired dogs it was good my mother was so happy it was like so much presser and anxiety had just disappeared it was like a new ma-ma but like the old ma-ma had reappeared it was good for my soul to see her so happy, relaxed, continent? I don't know but I do know it was a good thing ma-ma paddle around with me all day until I got on that plane and when I got to the airport it was a bitter sweet thing I wanted to stay with her and I was happy for her I didn't want to leave her but at the same time I could see the joy in her face.

My mother has never been so far away from me in my life and I know she is just a phone call away but I have gotten so use to her being close to me if I wanted to see ma-ma I was always just around the corner or just blocks away I can jump in my car and go see her in 20 minutes and I think that was the thing she didn't want for those that were wearing her down to be there with all of their problem and need and wants and still not a moment to live for her with having to raise all the grandkids that were left on her to raise like they were hers that was what she was running away from ma-ma was tired and wanted time to live for herself she had raised all 10 of us it was time out ma-ma needed space to find herself especially with daddy gone and I would never leave her to do things alone she could always call on me for help, advice whatever. She knew I would always be there to see about her and her needs and that Sophia and her kids were there also. I feel like my mother was run off from her own house she didn't care ma-ma wanted a change.

But I am so happy for ma-ma she stood up and made a change to make her life better for her. It take a strong person to leave what has been familiar to them all their life to go a strange new place start their life all over it take more than courage. that's when you know you are at a place in your life where your faith in god, preservation the determination in you heart is all you need because you know you are going to make it come hell or high water when you know you have giving your all to you family and now its' my turn my life to live for me now it's time to make that change. And ma-ma did give us her all she did love and raise us.

That's right she raised us all to the best of her abilities and some grand and I know she raised us very well. ma-ma don't owe us anything we owe her everything.

She gave us love unconditionally and hope she inspired us let us know that there isn't anything that we could not do. When needed ma-ma knew just how to stroke our ego. From the first time we tied our shoelace to that first A on the report card

Ma-ma made everything seam like a remarkable achievement because she did it all with love!

When I got back home my husband pick me up from the airport on the ride home we stopped to get food he wanted to sit and eat but I didn't because I was tired and not dressed I just wanted to get the food and go. When we got home we talked and ate he was more concern about ma-ma than I he had so many questions how do the house look? Is it far from Sophia? How many rooms does she have? Does she like it?

Baby don't worry I think ma-ma is very happy with her new home it is a very nice place she has enough room I don't think she needs or want 4 bedrooms she said if she had that many bedrooms then somebody will try to move in and she don't want that she said that if somebody wants to visit she has enough room for them but she don't want anyone staying with her.

She wants to live for her self by her self that's what she said.

The next morning when I got up the first thing I done was call ma-ma she didn't have her house phone on but her cell phone was on. When I got her on the phone I said: Hey ma-ma What you doing?

Nothing she said
What time is it she asks?
Its' 9: am I said

Well it's only 7: am here there is a two hour difference here
Chicago time is two hours ahead of us she said.
No wonder you sound like you were sleep.
Did I wake you up? I ask
No girl I was up making me some coffee so I could go out and
sit on my porch it's so nice and peaceful the weather is beautiful
baby I love my place I am so happy I feel so relaxed I haven't felt
like this in a long long time I thank you so much for driving me
here I thank god so much for you.
I know I can really count on you.

Ma-ma and I went on talking for about an hour but she
sounded so happy and relaxed to me but thru our conversation
I could tell she was really happy to get away from that house the
whole situation all you had to do was listen to her voice what
she was saying and you would know you could hear the shy of
relief I felt like it was a good thing that I was able to do this for
ma-ma.

Ma-ma and I would talk everyday 2, 3, 4, times a day when
I was no there with her. The next time I went there to visit was
in January and it was beautiful the weather the time spent with
ma-ma it was more than exceptional ma-ma looked so stress free
she was happy and now she had found her a thrift store that hit
the nail on the head ma-ma loved her some thrift store and she
had so much stuff from savers that was the name of the place she
wanted to go to savers everyday and she did her house was very
nice and quaint.
She had bought some things from savers and with the stuff
we brought from the house it made it complete although she

left a lot of things at the house. She did bring the bedroom set I had given to her a lot of other things but she did need a dinette set which she got from savers and some couches and that made the place complete she had everything else she wanted I stayed there for two weeks with her and Sophia and the kids I really enjoyed the time there with ma-ma and the rest of my family it was always hard to say bye but I knew I would be back so I would see them next time.

In February I was talking to ma-ma and she ask when you coming to see me?

I don't know ma-ma but it wont be long I don't have the money right now but I just left you. I said

So when you think you will be able to come? She asks

I can't say now but I do know I will be there to spend Mothers day with you. I said

Well I guess I will see you then she said.

Ma-ma and I continued our conversation with all the laughter and love we also shared some spiritual thoughts ending the call.

CHAPTER 7

Ma-ma and I continued to talk everyday on May 7ᵗʰ I left for Arizona I was excited to be going to see my ma-ma as was she to see me. now it was a Thursday I arrived there at 4:15 pm when I got off the plane I went to get my bags and walked out side so I could smoke a cigarette while waiting on Sophia and her husband to pick me up I began to talk with a lady and in the mist of our conversation Sophia droved up and said hey lady. I looked and I said to her what are you doing driving my car? But in a joking way but I was looking for them to pull up in their own car but no matter. Her husband got out of the car to greet me and put my bags in the trunk and we were off.

We were so happy to see each other and were just talking away I ask where's ma-ma? Sophia said at the house waiting on you.

I was so excited I couldn't wait to get there I wanted to see ma-ma Once we arrived I jumped out the car like a a you know how when you little and your ma-ma goes to work and drop you off at the babysitters and when she puts your coat on at the end of the day you know that meant only one thing that it was time to go with ma-ma! That's how I felt it was time to see ma-ma . . . I walked up to the door and I knocked and called out to her ma-ma she opened the door and I stepped in and I looked her in the eyes and was so overwhelm with I don't know I was so happy to see my mother tears just began to stream down my face ma-ma was crying too I guess it was just joy we hug each other so tight it was good ma-ma then walked over to the couch while wiping her tears so no one would see that she was crying she sat down and I sat in the chair across from her and I started talking.

Hey ma-ma how you doing? It's so good to see you.

What were you doing?

Nothing I had fallen asleep waiting on you all to get here she said. I missed you so much

Well I am here now. I said

Look at ya'll both crying and trying to hide it. Ya'll some babies. Sophia said. Ma-ma how are you? You look well. tell me what's' going on with you. Tell me how you are doing for real is everything going good for you? I ask.

Yeah girl everything is fine I just love my place and the weather is good I don't have to be in cold Chicago weather and I got everything I need I'm doing just fine with a smile on her face. how is your husband ? Why didn't he come with you? Well ma-ma you know with his schedule he had to work and he is booked solid for the next month or so some of the he has 3 gigs in one day he is busy which I think is a good thing for him.

Sophia where is your brothers?

They coming I told them you were here she said

Ok let me call them so I called when I spoke to him he said that he and his wife were on their way they were in traffic so I ask him to call his brother and let him know that I was waiting on them at ma-ma's house he said ok. I ask ma-ma if she had any beer.

No I don't have any beer girl. Ma-ma said

Ok ma-ma I just ask because you know you always have some stash for us beer head kids. Ma-ma didn't drink but there was always something around the house incase for company so I walked in the kitchen to the refrigerator and looked inside and saw 3 bottles of champagne that had been around since 1978 or something like that daddy had bought them and it look like one somebody had tried to open and ma-ma must have stop them. I then took the bottle from the refrigerator and over to ma-ma and ask her while holding the bottle up can I open this? Ma-ma looked and to my surprise said yes go ahead drink it. My reply was for real! I said you could didn't I. ma-ma said

So I opened the bottle and I poured myself, Sophia her husband, Marwin all of us some and we drank to ma-ma then I remembered that I didn't give ma-ma her mothers day gift I was going to wait until Sunday but I am glad I didn't.

So I ask Marwin to go out to the car and get my bag. When I got my bag I went inside and got ma-ma's gift and my camera I had bought her a diamond and blue sapphire bracelet and a hand carved jewelry box.

Ma-ma was very happy with her gift she gave me a kiss and a hug around the neck we went on from there as we sat around talking and drinking I started to record everything and it was a nice night. later that night we went to a club Sophia and her husband Marwin and his wife and my self ma-ma didn't want to go we went because the next day the 8 th of may would be Marwin's birthday him and his twin who was killed 2 years earlier so we went out to celebrate their birthday when we left the club it was late so I went to Sophia's house so I wouldn't wake ma-ma cause I didn't have keys I forgot them

The next day at about 9am I called ma-ma I ask her what she was doing and how she was doing. She said she was good and that she was going to come over to Sophia's house she was getting ready and ask did we have fun last night? I told her yes and that since she was on her was over to the house I would be waiting for her. I got a shower and dressed and ma-ma hadn't got there yet so I called her and she said she had stopped at savers and to pay her phone bill. So I told her I would come over later.

Sophia came into the kitchen. Good morning.

Good morning I said to her you look like you had a rough one. I said

Girl it was. You and Marwin dancing last night I thought I would fall off my seat. I got all your moves on my phone I recorded all that what ya'll thought ya'll were on soul train? Or was it the drinks? Ha-ha-ha said Sophia

Marwin is having a splash party at his house today. Are you going?

I just got off the phone with ma-ma and I told her I would be there. What time does the party start? I ask

I think he said to be there at 8:pm Sophia said

Well I can go to ma-ma's and we will come to his house later let me call her so I did just as I was about to get in the car with Sophia Marwin call me and ask if I could come over and help him get things together and he wanted me to cook I said ok but I was trying to find a way to be all the places I needed to be at once I was spreading my self thin so I called ma-ma back and told her I was going to go to marwin's house and do what I can to help him and if she could would she come over to his house he didn't live that far from ma-ma she said that she would meet me over there.

It was about 3:oclock when I got to his house then we needed to go to the store and get a few things when we got back to the house we had to go back to the store because we had forgotten the meats so now we go back to get the meats then I start to prepare the burgers and the salads stakes and the chips and dips and the mixed then I tell marwin to get the fire started on the grill and he don't have enough charcoal so this time I let him go to the store by this time people start to arrive Xavier and his girl Wayne some of Sophia's kids a few marwin's friends from his job marwin's girl was already there then ma-ma came with my sisters daughter ma-ma came in and sat on the big chair which was facing the door but it covered the whole room so see could see things later Sophia and her husband and the rest of her family arrived so we locked the front door and moved out to the pool area so everybody is enjoying their self and now I pull out my camera and I am just taking pictures of everything and everybody me ma-ma and Sophia's husband are all sitting at table and I am drinking some beer and he is too ma-ma has a pop and we are just laughing and watching the people enjoy Their self and I was so busy taking pictures of everybody all the kids not once did I think to just turn to my right and take a few of my mother or Lawayne or have some one take my picture never the less the evening was a success.

Ma-ma and I walked back inside the house and she sat in the same chair and I ask her if she wanted something to eat at first she said no but then she ask who made the burgers? I did

Then you can fix me one you know I don't be eating everybody's cooking. Ma-ma said

I know ma-ma I made most of the food do you want me to fix you a plate? You know what I will fix you a plate and you just eat what you want what ever you don't want we'll just throw it away ok I said

Ma-ma nodded her head to say yes

About an hour later after ma-ma had teased everybody there she said she was tired and she was going to go home and she would meet me at the house and she wanted to sit under her air conditioner see I can do those things now Ha-ha-ha.

Ok—ma-ma I will see you later and my sisters daughter went with her I could fell what ma-ma was talking about the temperature was 107 that Friday I ask her to call me when she got home and she did. we talked for a while after that I told her I loved her as I always did a little while later the party thins out and I leave with Sophia and her family I don't have a car so I went back to her house and we sat around on her patio and I told her I was suppose to go over to ma-ma house she said ok when Lawayne comes back you can take the van but you know the brakes are bad that's why we came to pick you up from the airport in granny's car.

Now time past and Sophia the kids and I are just sitting and talking, telling jokes just enjoying each other company and I decided to have another beer.

By the time he gets back I am a little tipsy and I don't want to drive and he didn't want to drive me. I have been nonstop since I landed so I decided to sleep there I got 2 whole weeks to be here and I will go to ma-ma in the morning.

Now I wake up its' Saturday morning and I go to the kitchen and put on the kettle to make some tea then the kids start to trickle in as if to keep an eye on me. when I made my tea I called ma-ma we talked then I told her I would be on my way as soon as I got dressed. then on of the kid that was standing near by ask I thought you said you were going to take us to Coaster and castles today?

When did I say that? I ask

Last night they all said like they were signing in a choir

Then I remembered I did say that. now I am thinking can I put it off but tomorrow is mothers day and I want to spend time with my mother like I want too and I don't want anything in my way I have been here 2 days and I am trying to be here for all my family that is here and I am excited to see everyone especially my mother I am spreading my self really thin so how do I do this I don't want to disappoint any one and I am not going to pull my mother out of the equation some one else will have to be understanding I don't want to do the babies either.

Let me think ma-ma I will call you back later after giving it some thought since Sophia's brakes don't work good on her car and kenny's car is to little to fit half of us and Xavier's car I can just count him out. Then a light I can get ma-ma's car and then she can go with us that's what I will do now how am I going to get to her ? I called Kenny to come and take me to ma-ma's house he came right away when he arrived there was Xavier with him. I was surprise to see him at Sophia's house since they have not been Seeing Eye to eye but I didn't say any thing and it seem to be cool but when I went back in the house because I forgotten something and Xavier came in behind me things got a little crazy but were quickly and easily contained. So we got in the car and drove over to ma-ma's house when we got there we all went inside Kenny and Xavier gave ma-ma a hug and said hello and sat for a while then I talked with ma-ma for a while then I ask her ma-ma why don't you come and go with us?

Girl how in the world do you think all of us are going to fit in the car? She said

We can make it work I said

Well look just take the car and take the kids where ever ya'll going I will see ya'll when ya'll get back ma-ma said

Are you sure? I ask

Yeap I don't feel like all those kids right now gone have fun ma-ma said

She reached in her purse and gave me the keys I said ok then gave here a kiss and started for the door ma-ma follow close behind when I walked out to the car ma-ma stood in the door way with the oddest look so I ask her what was wrong ?

Nothing she said.

Ok I said and I drove off and turn the car around and ma-ma was still standing in the door I stop the car and ask what ma-ma what do you need do you want something? She said no and wave goodbye as I drove off. Now I go back to Sophia's house to get all the kids when I got there the kids were all ready and waiting soon as I pulled us they came running from every where I told them to get in the car as I went into the house to let Sophia know that we were about to leave. she then walked out to the car with me her or her husband didn't go with me it was just me and 11 kids but it was fun as soon as I found the place it was a enormous place with all sorts of rides and video games and a few VR game.

The place was so big I got a little bit nervous because I had so many kids with me and I didn't want anything to happen to any of the kids or lose one of them so I had to give my firm lecture and stand really firm on it because the kids will get really excited and kind of jump around a little bit and a place like that is a predators' playground but not on my shift.

Once we were all inside and the rules were laid we broke off into groups but I kept my eye on them.

I got in on the action I played a few games there were all sort of games I can't name them all. It was a second floor also full of games stuffed animals and you cant forget the people once we left from there on went on the outside it was like the biggest amusement park I had ever seen.

The kids and I walked around and they did a few rides and soon it was time for us to go.

On the ride back I stopped at Diary queen and got us all ice-cream then we started on our way back to the house I only know two ways to get back to the house while driving the kids and I were talking they were excited and I think they really enjoyed their self's but now I missed my turn but thank god I was driving on Indian School Rd. because that street takes you all the way thru one side to the other and I didn't want to get lost with all these kids so I just keep straight and then things get filmier to us all now I get directions from them but at this point I know where to go.

I drive up to Sophia's house and we all get out then it hit me I didn't go to ma-ma's that's because I had all the kids and I knew they all belong to Sophia after I missed my turn to ma-ma's house my mind was just one track take the kids back where they belong. Sophia and her husband were sitting outside when we arrived and I sat and started talking then I had a beer with them while calling ma-ma I put her on speaker phone so Sophia could join in then I ask ma-ma what she was doing and if she wanted me to come and get here or stay over there with her?

No she said I ask her what she was doing again

Nothing I just took a bath and I am going to cook those ox tails for tomorrow she said

Ma-ma you don't have to cook those ox tails I keep telling you tomorrow is your day and we are going to have fun it's Mothers day we are going to eat and do what ever you want I got it all planed I said

We laughed and talked some more then I ask ma-ma do you need anything? No she said

Do you want me to bring the car? No she said

Well if you need anything let me know because I am going to sit here for a little while then I will be there. I said

Then I ask what you going do ma-ma? You want us to come there? No she said are you sure? I ask

Yes I am she said

Ok ma-ma I will be there in a little bit love you

Love you too ok bye.

I sat with Sophia and we had another beer or two then I thought I am a little tipsy I cant drive like this so I went inside to relax for a bit before I start to drive to her house

Sophia came and woke me up and I ask aren't you going to grannies house I said yeah what time is it? I don't know but I do know it's after 11:00 and you have to go around because the first gate is locked it's locked every night at 10:00 so you can't go the way you always go. Well I don't know the other way I only know one way. Hold on said Sophia Wayne and I will go with you.

Once we got to the house ma-ma opened the door and we all walked inside and I looked at ma-ma I ask what's wrong she sat on the ottoman by her bed and said I cant breath!

What I yelled

And in the blink of and eye ma-ma just slumped over and that was it.

I screamed out ma-ma and I put her on the floor and I started to do CPR and at the same time I was yelling at Sophia to call 911 her husband ran out the room crying and I went into shock and I am working on ma-ma and still nothing happen she just left me I cant believe what I am seeing it can't be real I still can't believe it today . . . .

It took the paramedics 2 minutes to get there then they began to work on her but to no avail so now I start to call my sisters and brothers my little sister came to ma-ma's the paramedics had just left with her I was on my way behind them and I had lost the keys to the car.

I am blundering around in a daze looking for the keys and my sister and Sophia trying to help me it was just a nightmare

Suddenly the lady next door came out from her house and ask if everything was alright she had seen the peramedics and the fire department she ask if there was something she could do to help I ask her if she could drive me to the hospital she said yes we all got into her car and I ask her to keep an eye out on ma-ma's house until I could get back and she said yes I will do that for you. If someone else come to her house before you get back what should I do? She ask

Don't let anyone in and if you see any one trying to go in call the police I don't want any one there until I get back and find the keys. I said thank you so much

Now we go into the hospital and back to the room were ma-ma is and the doctors and nurses and some other people met us and stop us at the entrance stop us and ask who is the person in charge or something to that affect and my sister pointed to me the doctor began to say and before he could get the words out of his mouth I just lost it I felt it I knew what he was going to say I didn't want to hear those words I cant hear it my heart is pounding out of my chest and I just know those words are coming tears are running down my face uncontrollable my legs are shaking then he said it and I let out a scream like a banshee it's just something about the words being said you know the truth you can feel it in your whole being but it's just the confirmation that just shuts you down !

My sister burst into the room

Sophia took off right for the room screaming it was just chaos

I don't know what to do I just sit on the floor in the hall

I can't believe my mother is gone now what?

I don't want to do this again first my father then my son now my mother . . .

Not to mention the hell I will go through with my siblings I never put this into the equation

I try to gather my self just enough to call my brother's and sister the family to fill them in on the tragic news and none of my brothers answered their phone after several tries I left massages for them to call it was very important. Then I began to call other family members and no word from my brothers or sister then I just sit and try to get myself together because this is a hard thing to have to do I cant stop crying and my head is filled with so many things I need to do. How I am going to get my mother back to Chicago all her belongs the funeral home what she will wear the flowers the people everything and still no one called I just sit there in the hot sun not realizing it is really that hot drinking beer after beer and I cant stop crying . . . .

CHAPTER 8

Then Sophia and her husband take me over to his mother's house and it is mother's day to remind you. when we get there his mother offers me food and her condolences I can't eat but I did have a drink then while we were there I get a call at 5:30 pm which Arizona is 2 hours behind Chicago which makes it 7:30pm in Chicago it's my big brother and the first thing out his mouth is WHERE IS THE CAR? Not what happen or how you doing? Do you need something? Or how are you holding up or I am sorry you had to go thought this alone nothing like that just where is the car.

I cant believe this is coming from him with all that ma-ma has taught you how she raise us all up and given of herself I cant put this together where is the love what about ma-ma I cant even talk to him I try to keep it pleasant but I just lost it

Things got ugly real fast then I just hung up the phone . . .

Then at about 9:30 Chicago time I get another call from my other brother and I'll be dame if he didn't ask the same thing it seem to me that they didn't give a dame about any thing but self and the dame car!!!

I hung up the phone and went to sit down but I am so stressed out I just loose it I am crying all over the place I am on the ground Sophia and her husband are trying to help me then his mother come over to help I lost it I totally lost it I feel like my life has come to a close I don't know what to do where I am what is happening? Is this real it took me a while to get it together but once I did I maid up my mind and knew just from our conversation that I definitely I had to do this all by myself and I needed to do it for my mother something just took over me and I just snapped into action oh I did find the keys when I went back to ma-ma house then I began to gather all the important papers documents and I start to call places to get this thing done next I had to clear out the house next I had to get a ticket to for ma-ma and they told me she would be shipped as cargo? But first I had to pay for a funeral place there to say that she was dead and do what was necessary by law in order for her to be flown back to Chicago

I didn't have enough money because I had to pay for myself another ticket American Airlines wouldn't give me a heart ship ticket and they wanted to charge me $249.87 for cancelling my original ticket so it was cheaper to just buy another now I call my husband and ask him for the money for ma-ma but first I had to pay the funeral home in Arizona because if I didn't she wouldn't be moved to the funeral home in Chicago. He did a money transfer and that was done now I need to call the funeral home in Chicago to give them a update on where I am as far as progress then there was something else I had to do it went on and on . . . ..

From Sunday thru Wednesday the day I left for Chicago it was so much to do and I wasn't finished yet we were just on our way home at 6:10 am my mother and I were in the sky on the same flight only thing she was on the lower deck as cargo?

Can you imagine you mother the irreplaceable person that love you from the cradle into your adulthood bandage your knee rub your belly when it hurt gave you that extra push when needed and love beyond measure being called cargo?

Not me it doesn't feel right.

The plane landed at 10:45 am my husband was there waiting for me it was good to see him and feel him feeling what I am feeling and to get a hug a genuine hug.

Now I go home and I don't get a change to unpack my phone wont stop ringing the funeral home, family on bullshit, friends and people from the neighborhood wanting to help

Family from my husband side of the family doing all to help and I really appreciate them so much now I have to set dates and get

My mother set like the first Lady

That's what she is to me my first lady

I have to gather up my brothers and sisters to let them know my course of action and still no one offered anything.

Still I move forward

Now I have about 45 nieces and nephews plus other family members and I am getting bum rushed not to mention I have to go to the funeral home today and go over the things I want for my mother once I leave there I have to go to the flower shop and get flower arrangements.

Now get this my niece ask me if she could go to the funeral home with me I told her I didn't want her with me I could do this because I know how she can start shit out of nowhere and for no reason that's just her so she begged and I just said fuck it I let her come with me because I really didn't need no shit my patients were bad and I was working with a hair trigger.

She tried to kick some shit off but I cut her off at the pass and made her go out and wait in the car!! Once I finished I went out to the parking lot to get in my car so I could leave and go to take care of the rest of the business as I turn to the lot to get in my car stunned my car was not there neither was my niece she had took off with my car do you believe this shit?

Now I don't know what to think if she is going to come back with my car or if something happen or what so I just stand there for about 15 minutes no car. I'm mad I have a lot of stuff going on inside of me I don't want to hurt her but I am thinking when she pull up I am going to beat her senseless

Trying to keep my composure about myself then I see a police so I stop them and tell them what that my niece stole my car. See I left the keys in the car so she could listen to the radio and open the window I didn't think she would take my car.

But why didn't I that's her character but I just didn't think she would do that to me I wasn't thinking too clear on this day anyway.

The police called it in and drive off to start to looking for my car 2 minutes later her she comes I was so mad I flung open the door and pulled her out I was about to hit her I ask her why did she do that ?

Then I told her that's alright just get out of my car and get home the best way you can. I left her standing right there in the street and I drove off

Because of that I didn't make it to the flower shop before they had closed so now I have to go tomorrow so now I turn around and head to the printing shop to get the obituaries made after that I head to Damen so I could let my family know where I am at as far as progress and still no one offer a thin dime I didn't say anything and didn't ask for anything.

Once I get to the house my husband greet me ask how did things go do you need anything? He ask no I am fine things are moving along. We sit on the porch and we have a cigarette and talk for a while.

Then he had to go to work he ask if I wanted to come so I wont be in the house alone but I said no I just didn't feel like it my heart and mind was very heavy.

I would not have made good company for any one.

I had a lot of calls coming in family and friends looking for information about ma-ma services then I got a call from the funeral home asking me to bring the clothing that I wanted ma-ma to be dressed in.

I told them I would bring them in the morning

Now I am on my way to the funeral home and I get a call from my brother and he ask why you didn't meet us so I guess you wasn't going to come and meet us anyway? I am lost I don't know what the hell he is talking about Then I hear my niece in the background saying I told ya'll she wasn't going to be here just hang up. Some kind of way I heard the funeral home mention so I say to him ok I am on my way. Now when I get there none of them are there but my big brother is there with his wife I look at him I ask him what's going on? Do you know this little shit starter has told them that I didn't do right by my mother I only spent $ 2.000 dollars on my mother I didn't get a funeral car a lot of lies I guess this was a way to get back at me because I made her walk home after she stole my car now she done told them this shit and they went over there listening to her and made their selves look like fools now I really want to beat her ass but my big brother had enough sense to wait for me to get there so he could see the paper work for his self when he did he told me I did a good job and he didn't know what to think but he do know my niece and all the lying, bullshit, troublemaking she do that's why I waited for you. Just keep doing what you are doing.

I give them the clothing for ma-ma and left I went to find my niece I couldn't find here she hid from me until the day of the service I saw her sitting in the church but it's alright I didn't say a word she know what she did . . . .

Now I try to keep everything together the service, the family as much as I could. My sisters and brothers played me like I had did something wrong like I had kill their child or something none of them sat by me or said a word to me and when it was time for the family to mingle with the people and say a prayer and break bread none of them came into the dinning area. My husband and my baby brother were by my side friends, family, and all the neighborhood supported me.

Then we went to the house and there were people there for as far as you could see the house, porch, the lot was full everyone was waiting for me with hugs and kisses and kind words at this point I guess it started to bug them how they were acting so then they began to talk to me I didn't feel it was genuine never the less I didn't say anything instead I just receive them.

As the night went on and some of the people began to go I sat on the porch and talked with my family and explain to them my plan of action with the house and everything that was left to me and that it would take me some time first I had to be clear minded to do any thing in the mist of everything they just started acting like just dam fools . . . gimme me this . . . gimme me that . . . . you owe me this, what you should do then they just want to fuss and fight and argue not to mention all the shameful things they have done to ma-ma . . . .

It is so unbelievable to how they have changed to shame . . . .
I have heard talk of how drugs will change a person and I have also seen the dramatic change in a persons appearance but

to actually see the mental change it has on a person will leave you speechless and if it is someone you has grown up with and love it is devastating and you look at them in disbelief but at the same time you wonder why this person cant see the change in their self why they cant see what this shit has done to them or do they want to see?

Its' a real sad thing how do you help someone like that where do you start? How do you help someone that won't help their self? And don't really want you to help unless you are willing to contribute to their cause. Why would I do that?

I am at a lost they are killing their self I don't know what to do I just keep praying.

It's like their pride won't let them admit their status of where they are in life and it's because of choices that they are there. not the up brining not the parents and in this case defiantly not because of lack it's as simple as CHOICE! That's it no one made that choice but them they did it and only they can undo it but it's their choice I thought losing our parents would make them stand up and make that change but it seem like they went deeper because they don't have to explain or face ma-ma or daddy cause their not here anymore.

But what they should look at is they are still representatives of this clan and have enough love and respect for the people that raised you and guided you in life to want to do their best if not for them what about your children what about self? Doesn't it matter how they perceive you as a parent?

Anyway I got thru that and I went home it was hard for me about a week later the service was held for my mother I think I really did a good job I know ma-ma would have been pleased.

There were a lot of people at the service it was a really sad time for me.

I don't remember a lot of the things that were done or said during the service but I do know that my sibling weren't nice to me at all once except one of my brothers . . . we arrive at the cemetery I walked over to see my daddy's head stone and said a few words then I went back over where ma-ma rest once we left the cemetery and got back to the church so the everyone could eat none of my family came in they didn't participate for what ever reason I don't know

I do know they didn't walk with me or talk to me but it was ok I went to the house and all the people were gathering there on the side of the house in our lot there were so many people talking to me coming at me from every direction after about 2 hours of this my family seemed to start to come around but it felt to me like too little too late and it hasn't been that good to date. I still love them and pray for them everyday.

We some times talk on the phone a bit but nothing to solid I wish I could say that something great came from their death like a street named after daddy or a dedication to ma-ma or the family found this strong sense of unity but I can't say that

Because none of that happen

It just seem like the family got more astringed and I still love them but I find it much easier to just let them live their life and love them from a distance hoping to fine that middle place. There is some good that came from my parents is they added 4 generations all of strength and prosperity!

With this my parent's legacy will live on. I cant say that this has been an easy journey but it has been one of strength, development, and faith for me what it has done for me is build my faith in God I told you about my daughter and the battle she had to go thought with the cancer now after her surgery which the doctor said was the cure about 3 months later she began to get sick and has been in the hospital about 25 times to date. Now this shows how God conditioned me all of this just gave me the strength that he knew I would need to get though this and to give her faith and keep her children in faith today she is fine and healed in Jesus name and that is only a blessing from god with all we went though the doctors saying they didn't know they couldn't find nothing but yet in still she just falling out any time any where getting sick without a cause but it is ok God fixed all of that in Jesus name

A lot of times we go though a lot of stuff in life and the first thing we want to do in responds to it is fuss but what we don't see is there is a reason we go though it all we are being made ready for something God knows that we will need extra strength to bear it what ever it might be.

I lost my father, my son, my business, my mother, my job and God just knows another loss at this time would not be good for me. That's why I just love and praise him.

I do know that God said (cast your cares on me for I care for you) and I walk by his word.

Now time has passed and I don't see my family that much because they are all over the states but some are still here in the city. But we still don't see each other on a daily basis but talk via the phone. I still have loose ends to tie up the house for one which I have my brother living in and he hasn't tried to get his self together and find a place and it is hard to sell property in Englewood no one wants to by because of the area and the bad part of that is this is good property in a undesirable neighborhood the ones that are interested are trying to rob you without a gun like a person don't know the value of what they have.

I have divide things amongst my sibling no matter what you cant make they happy because they still worried about what the next person has if it is two dollars more than what they got which is dumb to me well I have come to learn you cant please all the people all the times no matter what you do somebody is going to be mad so I just try to do the right thing I don't mean to hurt anyone so I just try to be fair and do the right thing there is nothing else to do . . .

There are so many things to do some of which weren't an easy fix and that took a lot of time to get fixed.

Now of all this I am still trying to get things done and I still have a couple of siblings that are doing things to block me and I don't understand why every time I talk with one or the other I get asked when are you going to sell the house ? But all the time they are waiting for my responds just to see what I would say knowing all the time they tried to run interference. Doing cunning tricks to block me but I think at this point they have realized that it is no way around it they have to stop with all this trickery and let me do what has to be done it's the only way to move forward in this.

CHAPTER 9

Now that I have come to terms with the fact that I have to accept the fact that my parents are no longer here things were left on me to do the right thing maybe I was looked upon as being the only responsible one or the person to be trusted I don't know but I do know I have more responsibilities now as being the go to person for my family

I have asked God to help me to forgive them. I know that they are not at their best and don't know what they are fully doing just acting out of hurt, pain or denial but what ever it is I still love them I know they will come around I don't know when I pray it will be soon.

As of today we are in a clam period and things are just going

I am still waiting on a sale for the house trying to keep all bills to a minimum at both my house and there I don't have a lot of money but I do what I can

I can see that it is becoming a little to much for my husband but in the mist of the hand life deals you I can't just give up I have to put my trust in God and really press forward looking and hoping for the best. life is not going to be all peaches and cream there are a lot of bumps all along the way things might not go the way you want them too if life worked that way we would never suffer lost of anything or anyone but it don't work like that we hear life is what you make of it sometimes that can be true but only if you make the right choices and accept that we are not in control we have to respect a higher power and in that know that we do have choices to choose the wide or the narrow road it's strictly up to you what you do.

To know that at a time there are things and people that has to be moved to make us stronger and set us in a different direction so that we can get to that place in life. All that don't kill you only makes you stronger in this life we need strength just to get from one day to the next.

I don't have all the answers I have been though so many trials in my life I had to get strength form somewhere other than myself because with just me I don't think I would have made it when I look in my family my marriage my financial status and the loneliness the sacrifices I have made in life to denied self and step out on faith Just cause I know it was God that gave me strength. As for today I am good and things are looking up and I see nothing but prosperity in my path success in all areas of my life I can do all things though Christ who strengths' me. There were days when I couldn't do nothing but cry a lot of things I didn't understand the rhymes and reasons the whys. I wanted to give up but couldn't so many people in life depending on me yet they don't realize it. Not saying if it was not for me or patting my self on the back but instead that I am glad that I made the right decision.

I don't worries about what people say or do it's going to always be something wrong with what you do or say if left up to people dame if you do dame if you don't especially if it is not their way. We can't go though life people pleasing that don't work because it is impossible we can't look for someone else to make us happy we have to do that for ourselves then share happiness . . . .

Then you will find that's what works.

I really miss my parents a lot of times I think let me call them and then I realize I cant sometimes I see a certain program on T.V and I think of them like when I want to call them and say hey ma-ma, daddy I have just written another book, I am in college, all sorts of things in a days run and I can only wish they were still here like when I think about when daddy would give me pointers in life when ma-ma would say be careful what you say. All the things about how you would carry yourself as a lady the warm talks when she had to knock me on my butt how I would love to rewind those times ma-ma, daddy good friends of mine. In our life we have people that mean so much to us it is impossible to put in word the true value of what they bring to our life. We look at them and in our minds we believe that they would be here forever we just don't see it like someday they would be gone and when this happen when they go to be with God there is a pause in our life. What has actually happen is they have just moved to a higher way of living. Which now we have to graduate to get to the place of a higher living we can't stop living here we must go on even though it is hard I want to graduate. don't you?

There are a lot of people that know just what I am talking about. Some of you have probably gone though worst than I. The bad thing about this kind of sibling reverie is most people don't want anyone to know of it not even their closest friend because of the embarrassment. Yes embarrassment and the lies they will tell to make you look like the bad guy. When you hear about the things that are being said it hurts you because you don't want to believe what you are hearing then you ask yourself why would they say the things they are saying. Now you have all kinds of emotions flying though your head and heart.

When you reflect back on all the things, secrets, pacts, life you have shared with them you just wonder why? You wonder is it money? They could have ask, is it jealousy why? Hate, or is it their way of dealing with the lost? Seeing the place they are in at the time of the lost. Maybe it's the anger they have against their self and need to put the blame on someone else?

I could go on guessing with never reaching the truth. The fact of the matter is that this happen and it is a real thing that people just don't deal with. Some never resolve this and haven't spoke with family members in 20 years and don't even know why. And it does not make sense by the time you come to terms with them it's too late that persons health has fail them. Or it's just to late for them now you have to live with the fact that you didn't fix the misunderstanding now you let this pick at your mind for God knows how long. Will you let this take you into bad health?

No fix it talk until you get it right most of the time people don't really mean it they just let pride get in the way. And will not be the first to say I am sorry and we not wanting to be the first so it never gets said. Why spend years like this years you could be enjoying and reminiscing. Why loose precious moments life is to short didn't you learn that from your past experience hug somebody, call somebody love somebody we need too . . . .. .

Some times we even have to pray about things we don't understand and there are things people yes even family will say things we don't know why they are saying them. It hurts it cuts deep and still we live. We need to get over it and let bygones be bygones Hell if we cut off everyone that has lied on us this would be one miserable place to live. Everybody needs love.

It really amazes' me how someone can go from sugar to shit you know like someone you went to school with you grew up in the same neighborhood shared families then you move out of the neighborhood and come back and see this person and your mouth fly wide open and when you see the things they are doing you are stunned and in disbelief.

Now imagine it's you brother, sister, your family what do you do? How do you react to something like that? With all you do to help them help their self to get better and to no avail it seems as if they like where they are just stuck and if you don't supply their need then you are not right you are against them if you let them tell it. But how can you help them ? Now with your parents watching the child they raised killing their self felling helpless and ashamed and taking care of them until they die. You would think this would make them get it together. But no it's time to point the finger like someone did them wrong how can you trust them to take responsibility and do what needs to be done would you trust them?

All I can do is keep doing the right thing and be fair with them and pray pray pray and believe that they will get it right. When a believing person prays, great things happen (James5:16)

Now all I can say is that I can't believe the change that has happen in my family. Where did all the love go all the things my parents instilled in us all the talent, skills the trust it's like shells where a people use to be. It's all about a hustle not living real life they have changed so much so distance from the person they were meant to be a complete change. The shameless being they have come to be no consciences about anything just do what I have to in order to get what I need for the moment just living day to day . . . . It is a very sad thing that there are people that think and live like this. This is there expectances of life no future plans for live just day to day.

There is one thing I have to keep focus on that is to not let society dictate to me what life is or isn't what should or shouldn't be not to conform to the world's way of thinking. I have learned if someone has been mean to me I don't have to treat them mean. This will allow me to have peace in my life. I am not made to be changed by the world but instead to make a change in the world. I had to recognize I have the power it's in me a gift from God. We are supposed to be leaders not followers. And if we choose to follow the world and become full of strife, spitefulness, jealousy, invenious and never understanding then . . . .

This is a change a drastic change . . . . A change to shame

Everything I do shell prosper (Psalms 1-3)
In Jesus name Amen